AT YOUR SERVICE

English for the Travel and Tourist Industry

Trish Stott
Angela Buckingham

OXFORD UNIVERSITY PRESS

OXFORD
UNIVERSITY PRESS

Great Clarendon Street, Oxford OX2 6DP

Oxford University Press is a department of the University of Oxford.
It furthers the University's objective of excellence in research, scholarship,
and education by publishing worldwide in

Oxford New York

Auckland Cape Town Dar es Salaam Hong Kong Karachi
Kuala Lumpur Madrid Melbourne Mexico City Nairobi
New Delhi Shanghai Taipei Toronto

With offices in

Argentina Austria Brazil Chile Czech Republic France Greece
Guatemala Hungary Italy Japan Poland Portugal Singapore
South Korea Switzerland Thailand Turkey Ukraine Vietnam

OXFORD and OXFORD ENGLISH are registered trade marks of
Oxford University Press in the UK and in certain other countries

© Oxford University Press 1995

The moral rights of the author have been asserted

Database right Oxford University Press (maker)

First published 1995
2009 2008 2007 2006
10

No unauthorized photocopying

All rights reserved. No part of this publication may be reproduced,
stored in a retrieval system, or transmitted, in any form or by any means,
without the prior permission in writing of Oxford University Press,
or as expressly permitted by law, or under terms agreed with the appropriate
reprographics rights organization. Enquiries concerning reproduction
outside the scope of the above should be sent to the ELT Rights Department,
Oxford University Press, at the address above

You must not circulate this book in any other binding or cover
and you must impose this same condition on any acquirer

Any websites referred to in this publication are in the public domain and
their addresses are provided by Oxford University Press for information only.
Oxford University Press disclaims any responsibility for the content

ISBN-13: 978 0 19 451316 6
ISBN-10: 0 19 451316 5

Typeset in Palatino and Helvetica

Printed in China

ACKNOWLEDGEMENTS

The authors would like to thank the students and staff at Tokyo Air Travel
College for their assistance during the piloting of this book

*The publishers would like to thank the following for their time and
assistance*: Experience Books, Sydney; Eckersley School of English

Cover photographs by: Art Directors; James Davis Travel Photography;
Zefa Picture Library (UK) Ltd

*The publishers would like to thank the following for permission to reproduce
photographs*: Colorific!; Philip Dunn; Eye Ubiquitous; Greg Evans
International; The Image Bank; James Davis Travel Photography; Japan
Airlines; Japan National Tourist Office; Life File Photographic Library;
Oriental Hotel, Bangkok; Singapore Airlines; South American Pictures;
Tony Stone Images; Zefa Picture Library (UK) Ltd

Location photography by: Rob Judges

Illustrations by: Gary Andrews; Matthew Bell; Phillip Burrows; Paul
Dickinson; Ian Moores; Geo Parkin; Technical Graphics Dept, OUP

Contents

UNIT		FUNCTION	
1	May I introduce myself?	Greeting guests Introducing yourself Saying where people are from Making a short welcome speech	4
2	What do you do?	Asking people about their jobs Talking about jobs and workplaces	8
3	What time does the next train leave?	Asking about the time Telling the time Talking about timetables	12
4	What kind of room would you like?	Making a room reservation Completing reservation details Requesting information politely	16
5	Don't leave your bags on the bus	Giving instructions politely	20
6	Is there a bank near here?	Giving and understanding directions Saying where things are	24
7	Who's calling, please?	Answering the telephone politely Giving information politely Asking for information Taking a message	28
8	Would you like a window seat?	Asking people to do things Understanding and dealing with tourists' requests	32
9	How was your day?	Talking about the past Asking someone about their day	36
10	Are you ready to order?	Greeting restaurant guests Taking orders Understanding orders	40
11	How will you be paying?	Talking about money Asking about payment Changing money for someone	44
12	We'll meet back here at three o'clock	Explaining plans and itineraries to a tour group Answering common questions asked by tourists	48
13	Why don't you take the city bus tour?	Making suggestions and recommendations Describing tourist attractions	52
14	Shall I send you a brochure?	Offering to help people Understanding and dealing with tourists' problems	56
15	I look forward to hearing from you	Talking about experiences Asking and answering interview questions	60

Tapescripts	64
Multilingual word list	78

1 May I introduce myself?

LISTENING

Listen to four dialogs. Write the dialog number next to the correct picture.

LANGUAGE STUDY

Look at the language we use to introduce ourselves.

Speaker A	Speaker B
Good morning. I'm Akira Kambara.	I'm Chris Bailey. Pleased to meet you, Mr. Kambara.
Excuse me. Are you Mrs. Lee?	Yes, that's right.
Hello, my name's Eduardo Vargas.	Pleased to meet you.
Hello, everyone! It's nice to meet you! Welcome to Bangkok!	

Practice the introductions with a partner. Use your own names. Check your pronunciation!

Remember!
Good morning, *Good afternoon*, and *Good evening* are common ways of saying *Hello*. But *Good night* is only used in the sense of *Goodbye*. It never means *Hello*.

LISTEN AND PRACTICE

Judy Wong is a tour company representative. She is meeting a tour group. Listen to the dialog. What does she say? Choose **a** or **b** in each pair below. The first one has been done as an example.

1 **a** Hi, everybody.
   (**b**) Good morning, everybody.

2 **a** I'd like to introduce myself.
   b May I introduce myself?

3 **a** I'm Judy Wong.
   b My name is Judy Wong.

4 **a** I come from Taipei.
   b I'm from Taipei.

5 **a** I'm the tour rep for Eastern Tours.
   b I'm the tour rep for East-West Tours.

6 **a** Welcome to Taiwan.
   b Welcome to East-West Tours.

Listen again and repeat what Judy says.

MORE PRACTICE

Practice saying the names of the countries shown on the map. Check your pronunciation with your teacher. Can you add any countries to the map?

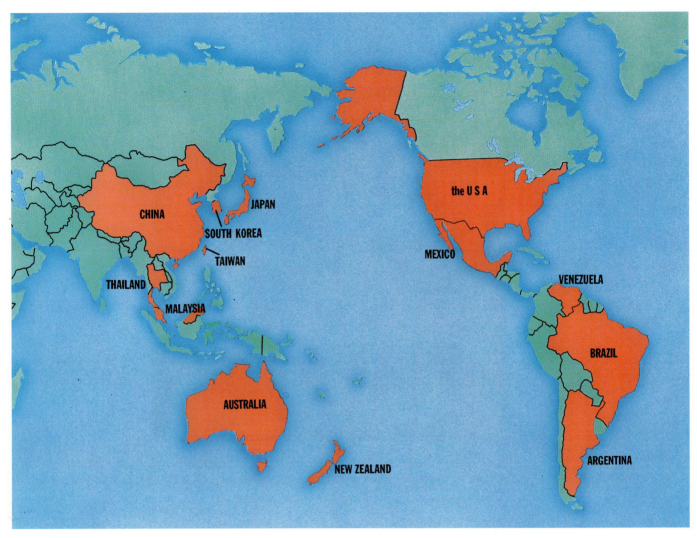

Now make sentences using the cues below.

Examples:

F Julie / Australia
Her name is Julie. She's from Australia.

M Mark / Ireland
His name is Mark. He's from Ireland.

F = female
M = male

1 F Berta / Mexico
2 F Elena / Turkey
3 M Roberto / Spain
4 F Judy / New Zealand
5 M Scott / the USA
6 F Miss Lim / China
7 M Mr. Yamamoto / Japan
8 F Ms. Kumat / Thailand
9 M David / the UK
10 M Ben / Australia
11 M Mr. Lee / Malaysia
12 M Mr. Kim / South Korea
13 F Ana / Venezuela
14 F Fatima / Egypt
15 M Victor / Argentina
16 F Ms. Chen / Taiwan

ACTIVITY You work for an American tour operator in one of its regional offices. Choose a card. You are meeting a group of tourists at the airport. Prepare a welcome speech.

Follow these instructions.
1 Greet the tourists.
2 Introduce yourself, and say which city you are from.
3 Tell them your job and which company you work for.
4 Welcome them to your country.

Work in small groups. Listen to each other. Then try the other cards. Check your pronunciation!

Masako Morita **Ambassador Tours** Naha, Okinawa, Japan	Miguel Martínez **Outbound Travel** México, D.F.
Alicia Díaz *Voyager Travel* Caracas Venezuela	Julia Lee **Universal Tours** Taipei Taiwan
Song Min Lee **Epic Tours** ★ Seoul South Korea	Shireen Lim **Atlas Travel** Singapore

SUMMARY Now you can
- Greet guests
  Good morning, everybody. Welcome to ...
- Introduce yourself
  I'd like to introduce myself. My name is ...
- Say where people are from
  She's from Ireland.
- Make a short welcome speech

Vocabulary

airport	introduction	tour operator
city	map	tour rep
company	meet	tourist
greet	tour company representative	welcome
introduce oneself	tour group	

2 What do you do?

LISTENING

Listen to five dialogs about jobs. Write the dialog number next to the correct picture.

☐   ☐

☐   ☐   ☐

LANGUAGE STUDY

Study these questions and answers.

Question	Answer
What do you do?	I'm a hotel receptionist.
What does she do?	She's a flight attendant.
What do they do?	They're waiters.
Do you work in a restaurant?	Yes, I do. / No, I don't.
Does he work in New York?	Yes, he does. / No, he doesn't.
Do they work in a hotel?	Yes, they do. / No, they don't.
Are you a waiter?	Yes, I am. / No, I'm not.
Is he a bellhop?	Yes, he is. / No, he isn't.
Are they receptionists?	Yes, they are. / No, they aren't.

Work with a partner. Take turns asking and answering questions about the pictures in the Listening.

Now ask and answer questions about these pictures.

waiter

tour guide

bellhop

you

tourist information officer

LISTEN AND PRACTICE

Listen to the dialogs and complete the sentences.

1 A What do you do?
  B I'm a _____ .

2 A _____ a bellhop?
  B No, _____ . He's a _____ .

3 A Where _____ ?
  B In a hotel. I'm a _____ .

4 A _____ a travel clerk?
  B _____ . I work in New York.

5 A Do you work in a _____ ?
  B No, _____ . I work in a tourist _____ office.

Listen again and repeat. Check your pronunciation!

Now practice the dialogs with your partner.

MORE PRACTICE

With your partner, make questions and answers using the cues below.
Examples:

You and Eduardo? / bar / Cancun? (Yes)
A *What do you and Eduardo do?*
B *We work in a bar.*
A *Do you work in Cancun?*
B *Yes, we do.*

Akiko? / airport / Japan? (No)
A *What does Akiko do?*
B *She works in an airport.*
A *Does she work in Japan?*
B *No, she doesn't.*

1. you? / hotel / Los Angeles? (Yes)
2. Ken? / restaurant / Hong Kong? (Yes)
3. Emily Wu? / travel agency / Taipei? (No)
4. Gloria and Miguel? / airport / Argentina? (Yes)
5. Yu-lin? / hotel / Hong Kong? (No)
6. you and Akiko? / tourist information office / Okinawa? (Yes)
7. she? / exchange bureau / Thailand? (No)
8. you? / restaurant / Seoul? (No)
9. Hiroshi and Mayumi? / bar / Tokyo? (Yes)
10. you and Enrique? / a tourist information office / Monterrey? (No)

ACTIVITY

These people work for an international company. They work all over the world!

Work in pairs. Play the *Who are you?* game.
Choose one of the people. Your partner guesses who you are. Take turns to ask "*Are you ...?*" and "*Do you ...?*" questions:

A *Are you a travel clerk?*
B *No, I'm not.*
A *Are you a receptionist?*
B *Yes, I am.*
A *Do you work in Mexico?*
B *Yes, I do.*
A *Are you Cecilia Cortez?*
B *Yes, I am!*

	Ana Vargas travel clerk Mexico		Nelson de Souza bartender Brazil	
Marie Lu receptionist Taiwan	Kyoko Sato receptionist Japan	Lidia Chang tour guide Taiwan	Sandra Pacheco travel clerk Brazil	Cecilia Cortez receptionist Mexico
Rik Lai bartender Taiwan		Clarisse Cabral receptionist Brazil		Mayumi Wada travel clerk Japan
	Marcos García tour guide Mexico	James Liu travel clerk Taiwan	José-Antonio Nogueira tour guide Brazil	
Masako Tanaka tour guide Japan		Kenzo Suzuki bartender Japan		Luis Martínez bartender Mexico

---

SUMMARY   Now you can
- Ask people about their jobs
  What do you do?
- Talk about jobs and workplaces
  I work in a hotel.

Vocabulary

bar	hotel	tourist information office
bartender (*or* barmaid)	receptionist	tourist information officer
bellhop	restaurant	travel agency
exchange bureau	tour guide	travel clerk
flight attendant		waiter (*or* waitress)

3   What time does the next train leave?

LISTENING

Write down the time you hear. The first one has been done as an example.

1 10:15   3 _____   5 _____
2 _____ 4 _____   6 _____

Now listen again and check your answers. Draw the times on the clocks below.

1   2   3   4   5   6

LANGUAGE STUDY

Look at the clock and examples below.

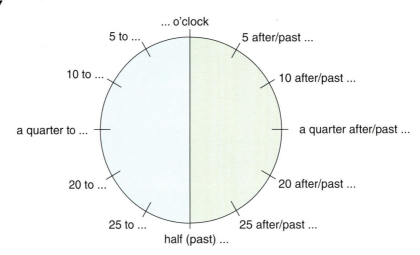

Examples: 2:15 = *two fifteen* or *a quarter after two*
           8:50 = *eight fifty* or *ten to nine*
           7:40 = *seven forty* or *twenty to eight*

Now practice saying these times.

Look at how we use *a.m.* and *p.m.*

a.m. = from midnight to just before midday
p.m. = from midday to just before midnight
Example:

7:15 a.m. = *seven fifteen a.m.* ✓
seven fifteen in the morning ✓
a quarter after seven in the morning ✓
≠ *a quarter after seven a.m.* ✗

LISTEN AND PRACTICE

Listen to the cassette. Match the pictures, verbs, and times. Draw a line. The first one has been done as an example.

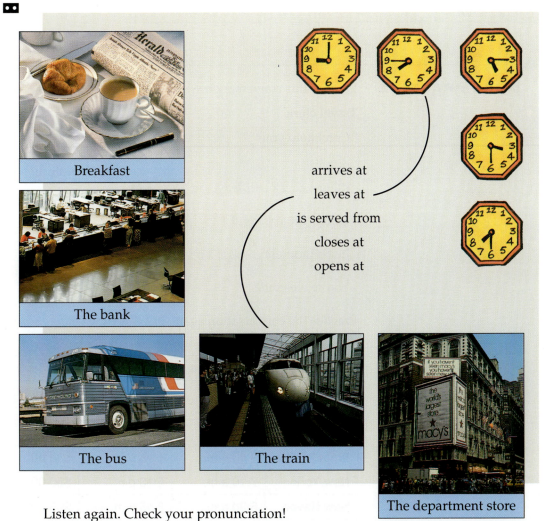

Listen again. Check your pronunciation!

Work in pairs. Take turns to make your own examples. Use the pictures below. Say your sentences to your partner. Check your pronunciation!

Example: *Lunch is served from 12:30 p.m.*

MORE PRACTICE

Practice this conversation with a partner.

Travel clerk

Can I help you?

I'll just check ... It leaves at **10:25** a.m.

Umm ... It arrives at **12:55** p.m.

Just a moment ... It's **$27**.

You're welcome.

Customer

Yes, please. What time is the next train to Baltimore?

And what time does it arrive, please?

I see. How much is a round trip ticket?

I see. Thank you very much.

Practice the conversation again, but this time change some of the answers. Use this information.

Timetable: Trains from Washington, DC				
To:	leaves	arrives	Prices ($)	
			one way	round trip
Baltimore	10:25 a.m.	12:55 p.m.	$14.00	$27.00
Philadelphia	9:40 a.m.	1:45 p.m.	$36.00	$70.00
New York	7:10 a.m.	5:15 p.m.	$50.00	$98.00
New Haven	6:30 a.m.	8:45 p.m.	$95.00	$188.00

ACTIVITY   Play this game in groups. Throw a dice and move your counter around the board. If you land on a clock, the person on your left must ask: *What time is it now?* You must answer the question.

If you make a mistake, miss a turn.

The first person to land on *Finish* is the winner!

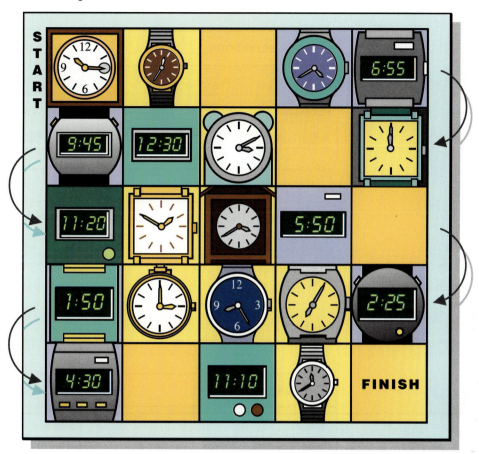

SUMMARY   Now you can

- Ask about the time
  What's the time?
- Tell the time
  It's nine fifteen.
- Talk about timetables
  The train leaves at ten twenty-five in the morning.

Vocabulary

afternoon	evening	morning	time
arrive	I'll just check ...	one way	timetable
bank	Just a moment ...	open	train
breakfast	leave	post office	
bus	lunch	round trip	
clock	midday	serve	
close	midnight	store	
department store			

15

4 What kind of room would you like?

LISTENING

Listen to three dialogs. For each dialog, check the card (**a** or **b**) with the correct information.

1 a ☐

Room reservations	
Name:	Baughan
Room type:	Single
Arrival date:	April 1st

b ☐

Room reservations	
Name:	Vaughan
Room type:	Single
Arrival date:	April 6th

2 a ☐

Room reservations	
Name:	Ms. Chang
Room type:	double with bath

b ☐

Room reservations	
Name:	Ms. Chang
Room type:	single with bath

3 a ☐

Reservation	
Name:	Mr. M. Stephens
Method of payment:	Traveler's checks
Reference number:	1234 567 890

b ☐

Reservation	
Name:	Mr. M. Stephens
Method of payment:	Credit card
Card number:	1234 567 890

LANGUAGE STUDY

Look at the questions we ask when we take reservations.

Receptionist	Guest
What's your name, please?	(It's) Smith.
When will you be arriving?	(On) April 4th.
For how many nights?	Two nights. / Until ...
What kind of room would you like?	A single/double room with bath, please.
How will you be paying?	By Visa/Access/American Express. Cash.
What's the card number, please?	It's 1234 567 890.

Practice asking and answering the questions with a partner.

LISTEN AND PRACTICE

First, fill in the blanks with questions from the **Language study**.
Then, listen to the dialog and check your answers.

A I'd like to make a reservation, please.

B Certainly, sir. _____ , please?

A Williamson, Bill Williamson.

B _____ , Mr. Williamson?

A July 12th.

B For _____ ?

A Until the 14th.

B So that's two nights.

A Yes, two nights.

B And _____ ?

A A single room with bath, please.

B And _____ , Mr. Williamson?

A By Visa.

B That's fine. _____ ?

A It's 0123 456 7890.

B And what's your address, please?

A It's 1738 Lincoln Drive, Washington, D.C. 26676.

B OK, Mr. Williamson, I can confirm your reservation. That's a single room for two nights from July 12th.

A Thank you.

Practice the dialog with a partner. Take turns being the clerk.

MORE PRACTICE

Work in pairs. Use the information in the dialog on the previous page to fill in the reservation form below. Then try to role-play the conversation without looking at the dialog. Take turns being the clerk.

RESERVATION FORM

Guest name:

Arrival date:

Number of nights:

Room type: ☐ single ☐ with bath
☐ double ☐ with shower

Method of payment: ☐ cash
☐ traveler's checks
☐ Visa ☐ Access ☐ Amex

card number:

Address:

Try the conversation again. This time use your own names, and change the other information.

WORD STUDY

Fill in the blanks to find the missing word.

1 Method of payment (4)
2 and 3 Another method of payment! (6, 4)
4 A room for one person (6)
5 Ask a hotel to keep a room for you (7)
6 The giving of money for services (7)
7 A room for two people (6)

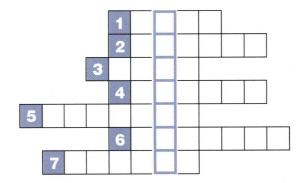

ACTIVITY Play this game in groups. You are reservation clerks in a hotel.

Throw a dice and move your counter around the board. If you land on a square marked **?**, you must ask the question politely. If you land on a square marked **!**, follow the instruction.

If you are right, go forward one square! If you make a mistake, miss a turn.

The first person to land on *Finish* is the winner.

Start	! Say today's date in English	Safe	? Ask the guest for his/her name	Safe
	Safe	? Ask the guest when he/she wants to stay	Safe	! Spell your name in English
	? Ask the guest about the type of room he/she wants	Safe	! Say your telephone number in English	Safe
	Finish	! Say your address in English	Safe	? Ask the guest about payment

---

SUMMARY Now you can

- Make a room reservation
  I'd like to make a reservation, please.

- Complete registration details
  What kind of room would you like?

- Request information politely
  What's your name, please?

Vocabulary

(credit) card number	confirm	night
... with bath	credit card	reference number
... with shower	date	reservation
address	double room	room type
arrival	guest	single room
cash	method of payment	That's fine.
		traveler's check

19

5 Don't leave your bags on the bus

LISTENING

Listen to the cassette. What are they talking about? Write the dialog number next to the correct picture.

LANGUAGE STUDY

Study these instructions.

> *Don't leave your bags on the bus.*
> *Write your name and address on this tag, please.*
> *Please check in at least two hours before departure.*
> *Please have your boarding pass ready.*
> *Have your passport and visa ready.*

If you are speaking to someone, giving instructions can sound too direct. So remember – always say "Please!"

LISTEN AND PRACTICE

Listen and complete these instructions.

1 _____ your bags on the tour bus.
2 _____ your name and address on this tag, please.
3 Please _____ at least two hours before your flight.
4 Have your boarding pass _____ .
5 _____ immediately to gate 37.
6 _____ leave any bags unattended.
7 Please _____ the plane through door E.
8 Fasten your _____ .
9 Do not _____ until you are inside the terminal building.
10 _____ your flight!

Listen again and repeat the instructions. Check your pronunciation!

MORE PRACTICE

Where would you see these instructions?

1 Press button to operate
2 Please do not disturb
3 Do not lean out of the window
4 Please check out before 11 a.m.
5 Ring for service

a At a reception desk
b In a hotel room
c Outside an elevator
d Outside a hotel room
e In a train

Now put the words in the correct order to make instructions for these situations.

6 not Do photographs take _____
7 the not on Do grass walk _____
8 off entering Take shoes before your _____
9 ticket the from machine your Buy _____
10 at key desk Leave front your the _____

21

WORD STUDY

Now you can give people instructions on how to use things – for example, public telephones. Look at the pictures below and fill in the blanks with these words:

Finally   First   Next   Then

(Check any new words in the **Word list** at the back of your book.)

_____ , pick up the receiver.

_____ , insert coins.

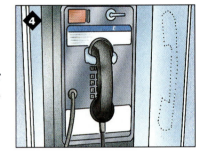

_____ , press the number you want.

_____ , when you finish your conversation, replace the receiver.

ACTIVITY

Play this game in pairs. Take turns tossing a coin and move around the board. Decide which side of the coin is "Heads" and which side is "Tails".

Heads = move one square.
Tails   = move two squares.

When you land on a square, look at the picture and say the instruction.
For example:

Do not take photographs.   *Please check in 2 hours before your flight.*

Look at the examples in this unit again if you need help. Use your imagination!

22

SUMMARY   Now you can

◆ Give instructions politely
Please fasten your seatbelts.

Vocabulary

at least	departure	outside	smoke
bag	elevator	passport	tag
board	enjoy	plane	terminal
boarding pass	fasten	put	through
building	flight	ready	unattended
check in	gate	reception desk	visa
check out	immediately	seatbelt	

6 Is there a bank near here?

LISTENING

What do these symbols mean? Match the words and symbols. One has been done for you as an example.

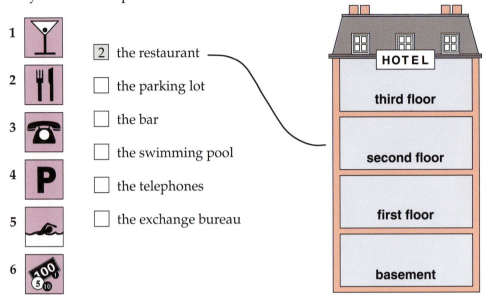

1.
2. ☑ the restaurant
3. ☐ the parking lot
4. ☐ the bar
5. ☐ the swimming pool
6. ☐ the telephones
☐ the exchange bureau

Now listen. Where is each place? Draw a line to the correct floor in the hotel, as in the example.

Work with a partner. Take turns asking and answering questions about places in the hotel.

Example:
A *Where's the restaurant, please?*
B *It's on the second floor.*

LANGUAGE STUDY

Study these pictures.

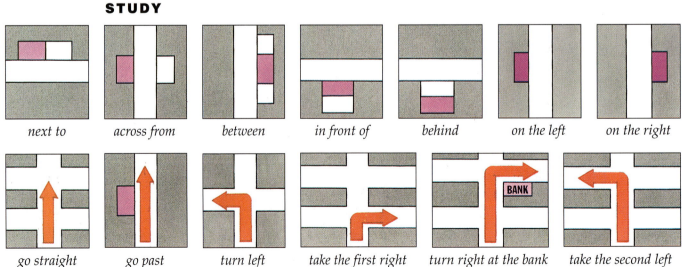

24

Now look at the plan of the shopping mall below and study these examples.

A *Where are the telephones?*
B *They are on the third floor, across from the elevators.*

A *Where is the exchange bureau?*
B *Go straight through the mall, past the fountain. It's on the left, across from the sandwich bar.*

LISTEN AND PRACTICE

Listen to the information clerk in the shopping mall telling people where things are. Where are these places?

1 the car rental office
2 the drugstore
3 the bus stop
4 the pizza parlor
5 the lost and found office

Listen and write a number on the plan.

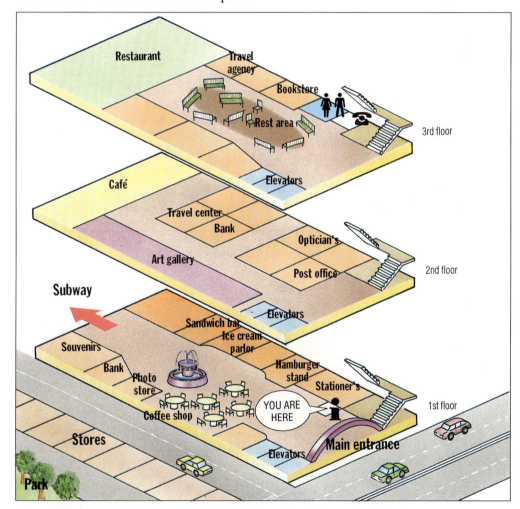

Work with a partner. Take turns asking and answering questions about places in the shopping mall.

Example:
A *Where's the bookstore?*
B *It's on the third floor, next to the restrooms.*

MORE PRACTICE

Look at this map of Sydney.

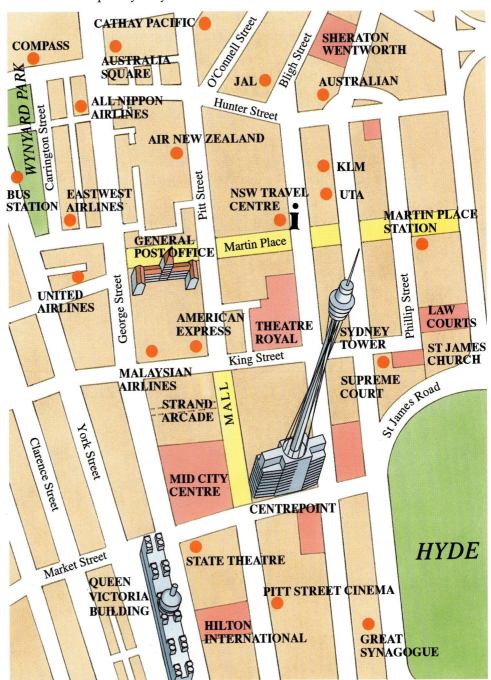

Source: Experience Books, Sydney

Match the tourists' questions with the answers on the next page. All the tourists are at Centrepoint. The first one has been done as an example.

1 Excuse me. How do I get to Wynyard Park from here?
2 Excuse me. Where's the Theatre Royal?
3 I'm looking for the New South Wales Travel Centre. Do you know where it is?
4 Can you help me? How do I get to Martin Place station from here?
5 Excuse me. Is the All Nippon Airways office near here?
6 Excuse me. Is there a post office around here?

☐ Well, go down Market Street and take the second right onto George Street. Go straight down George Street until you see it on your left.

☐ Oh, it's really near here. Turn left out of Centrepoint, take the first left, then go left again onto King Street, and it's on your right.

[1] Go straight down Market Street, take the third right and go straight down York Street. It's near the bus station, on your right.

☐ Yes. Turn right out of here, take the first right, keep going until you get to Martin Place, then turn left and you'll see it on your left. It's really big.

☐ Right. Go left down this street, take the second left, then the second right, and you'll see it in front of you on Martin Place.

☐ OK. Go left out of here, take the first left, then go straight across King Street. When you get to Martin Place, you'll see it on the corner across the street from you.

ACTIVITY Study the map again. In pairs, take turns asking for and giving directions. Ask three questions each. This time, your starting point is the General Post Office.

SUMMARY Now you can

- Give and understand directions
  Where's the exchange bureau?
  Go straight through the mall, past the fountain.

- Say where things are
  It's on the left, across from the sandwich bar.

Vocabulary

art gallery	excuse me	shopping mall
bookstore	fountain	station
bus stop	lost and found office	swimming pool
car rental office	main	telephone
corner	parking lot	theatre (US theater)
drugstore	restrooms	until
entrance		

7 Who's calling, please?

LISTENING

Listen to the telephone conversation and fill in the blanks.

A Good morning, Oriental Hotel, Bangkok. Can I help you?

B Hello. _____ to the General Manager, please?

A _____ he's not here at the moment. _____ a message?

B Yes, please. _____ Mr. Lopez, Roberto Lopez. _____ ask him to call me after 3 p.m. today?

A Certainly, Mr. Lopez. _____ your number?

B _____ 247 1033.

A Thank you. _____ him the message.

Day	Monday	Date May 17th	Time	10:15
To	General Manager			
From	Mr. Lopez			
Message	Please call him after 3 p.m. today.			
Tel No:	247 1033			

Listen to the cassette again. Work with a partner. Practice the dialog above with the same intonation as the voices on the tape. Take turns being the clerk.

LANGUAGE STUDY

Study this telephone language. Check any words you don't know in the **Word list**.

Receptionist	Caller
Good morning. Can I help you?	*Yes, please. Could I speak to Mr. Smith?*
Who's calling, please?	*This is Mrs. Jones.*
Could you spell that, please?	*It's J-O-N-E-S.*
One moment, please. I'll put you through.	*Thank you.*
I'm sorry. He's not here at the moment.	*Do you know what time he'll be back?*
I'm afraid he's in a meeting.	
I'm afraid he's on another line.	*Could I leave a message?*
I'm afraid the line is busy.	
Would you like to hold?	*Yes, please.*
Can I take a message?	*Yes. Could you ask him to call me?*
Certainly. Could I have your number?	*Yes, it's ...*

Work in pairs. Test each other! Cover the column on the right. Take turns reading the receptionist aloud. Can your partner remember the response?

When you have practiced all of them, change partners and try one more time.

LISTEN AND PRACTICE

Put the following sentences in the correct order to make a telephone conversation between a receptionist (R) and a caller (C). The first one has been done as an example.

☐ **R** I'm sorry. Mrs. Chang isn't here at the moment.

☐ **C** It's J-A-C-K-S-O-N. I'm staying at the Renada Hotel.

☐ **R** The Renada Hotel? Could I have your number?

☐ **C** Thank you. Goodbye.

☐ **R** Certainly, sir. Could you spell that, please?

☐ **C** Yes, it's 43 66 21.

☐ **R** I think she'll be back this afternoon. Can I take a message?

☐ **C** Could I speak to Mrs. Chang, please?

☐1☐ **R** Good afternoon. Minata House. How may I help you?

☐ **C** Yes, please. Could you ask her to call me? My name is Mr. Jackson.

☐ **R** Goodbye.

☐ **C** Do you know what time she'll be back?

☐ **R** Thank you very much, Mr. Jackson. I'll give her the message.

Now listen and check your answers.

Work with a partner. Turn to the tapescript on page 70 and practice the conversation. Check your pronunciation!

MORE PRACTICE

Work in pairs. Take turns being **A** and **B**. Practice the conversation below. If you need help, look at the **Language study** on page 29 again.

Student A You are a receptionist at the Plaza Hotel. Answer the telephone and take a message. Write it on the notepad.

Day	Date	Time
To		
From		
Message		

Student B Telephone the Plaza Hotel and ask to speak to Mr. Morrison. If you can't speak to him, leave a message.

Student A

Answer the telephone.
Good morning, Plaza Hotel. Can I ...?

Tell the caller that he is out of his room.
Ask if the caller wants to leave a message.

Ask for the caller's name and number.

Ask how the caller spells his/her name.

Tell the caller that you will give Mr. Morrison the message as soon as possible.

Student B

Ask to speak to Mr. Morrison.
Yes, please. Could I speak to ... ?

Say yes. Say that you want Mr. Morrison to call you.

Reply.

Reply.

Thank the receptionist and finish the call.

WORD STUDY Find the missing words. Use them to fill in the crossword.

Across
2 ☎
4 He'll be ... at four o'clock.
5 Person who answers the phone in a hotel.
8 She's on another ...
9 Could you ... him a message, please?

Down
1 Can I take a ...?
3 I'll put you ...
6 Could she ... me after five o'clock, please?
7 Could you ... your name, please?

ACTIVITY Use the information on the cards to make telephone conversations with your partner. Take turns being the receptionist. Don't forget to write down the message!

Ask for:	Mr. Wu
Your name:	Angela Carey
Your number:	491380
Message:	You want him to call you back.

Ask for:	Ms. Noya
Your name:	Enrique Sanchez
Your number:	597800
Message:	You want her to meet you at 7 o'clock, not 6 as planned.

Ask for:	Yoko Fujimoto
Your name:	Jitesh Patel
Your number:	870442
Message:	Tell her you'll call back later.

Ask for:	Rick Calderone
Your name:	Alice Huang
Your number:	997246
Message:	Ask him to call you back as soon as possible.

SUMMARY Now you can

- Answer the telephone politely
  Good morning. Can I help you?

- Give information politely
  I'm sorry. He's not here at the moment.

- Ask for information
  Could you spell that, please?

- Take a message
  Can I take a message?

Vocabulary

as soon as possible	caller	I'm sorry.
be back	certainly	line
busy	general manager	put somebody through
call	give a message	spell
call (2)	hold	take a message
call back	I'm afraid ...	

8 Would you like a window seat?

LISTENING

Angela is a Singapore Airlines check-in clerk. Look at the list of things she has to do when she checks in a passenger. They are in the wrong order. Try to put them in the correct order. The first one has been done as an example.

☐ Tell the passenger when the flight will start boarding.
☐ Ask if the passenger wants a window seat.
☐ Ask the passenger to put his/her bags on the scales.
1 Ask to see the passenger's passport and ticket.
☐ Ask if the passenger has any hand luggage.

Now listen to the dialog and check your answers.

LANGUAGE STUDY

Study these requests and responses.

Check-in clerk	Passenger
May I see your passport and tickets, please?	*Sure. Here you are.*
Could you put your bags on the scales, please?	*OK.*
Would you fill out this name tag and attach it to your bag, please?	*Sure. Do you have a pen?*
Can you go straight through to the Departure Lounge now, please?	*Yes. Thank you very much.*

Work in pairs. Test each other! Cover the column on the left. Take turns reading the answers aloud. Can your partner remember the polite request?

LISTEN AND PRACTICE

Listen to these conversations in a tourist information office between the clerk (**C**) and a tourist (**T**). Fill in the blanks.

Dialog 1

C Good morning. Can I help you?

T Yes, please. _____ to reserve two seats on the city tour today.

C Yes, certainly. _____ your name?

Dialog 2

C Good morning. May I help you?

T Can we leave our luggage here for 24 hours?

C Yes, you can. _____ fill out this form, please?

T Sure. Do you have a pen, please?

Dialog 3

C _____ I help you?

T Yes, please. I'd like to change some traveler's checks.

C Certainly. May I have _____ , please?

T I have my driver's license.

C That's fine.

Dialog 4

T Excuse me. _____ help me with accommodations?

C Certainly, madam. Could you _____ just wait until I finish helping this gentleman?

T No problem.

In pairs, take turns being the clerk and the tourist. Practice the dialogs.

33

MORE PRACTICE

Read the situation. What you would say? Work with a partner.
Examples:

You work as a travel clerk. You want a customer's telephone number.
May I have your telephone number, please?

You work in a hotel. A guest is checking in. You are not sure how to spell his/her name.
Could you spell your name, please?

1 You are an immigration officer. You want to see a traveler's passport.
2 You work in a hotel restaurant. You want a guest's room number.
3 A guest is paying by credit card. You want him/her to sign.
4 You work as a check-in clerk. You want a passenger to go to the departure gate now.
5 You are a tour guide. You want to talk to your tour group, but they are all talking to each other.
6 You are a flight attendant. You want a passenger to fasten his/her seatbelt.
7 You are taking a room reservation on the telephone. You want the guest's credit card number.
8 You work in a busy tourist information office. A tourist wants some information, but you are already helping someone.

ACTIVITY

Student A You work for a company that runs city tours. Help the customer (student B). Use the conversation plan. Look at the **Language study** (page 32) and **Listen and practice** (page 33) again if you need help.

Student B You are a tourist. You want to reserve a seat on the city tour. Use the conversation plan. Look at the **Language study** (page 32) and **Listen and practice** (page 33) again if you need help.

Student A	Student B
Ask the customer if you can help.	
	Say you want to reserve a seat on the city tour.
You want to know when he/she wants to go.	
	Say you want to travel today.
You want to know the customer's name.	
	Give your name.
You want the customer to spell his/her name.	
	Spell your name.
Ask the customer how he/she will be paying.	
	Say you will pay by credit card.
You want to know the customer's card number.	
	Give your card number (invent one!).
Confirm the reservation.	
	Thank the clerk.

Now try the conversation again. This time, ask different questions. You can use this list for ideas.

buses	car rental	trains	day trips/excursions
flights	shopping	weather	accommodations
restaurants	medicine	luggage check	money exchange

Example:

A *Can you give me some information about trains to Bangkok, please?*
B *Sure. Here is the timetable.*
A *Thank you. Also, please can you ... etc.*

SUMMARY

Now you can

- Ask people to do things

    Could you put your bags on the scales, please?

- Understand and deal with tourists' requests

    I'd like to reserve two seats on the city tour today.
    Yes, certainly. May I have your name?

Vocabulary

accommodations	fill out	passenger
aisle seat	form	reserve
check-in clerk	hand luggage	scales
city tour	help	sign
day trip	immigration officer	seat
departure lounge	luggage check	sure
driver's license	medicine	window seat
excursion		

9 How was your day?

LISTENING

Two tourists invite their Japanese tour company representative to dinner.
First, look at the sentences below. Check any words you don't understand in the **Word list**.

Then listen to the conversation. What do they say? Choose the correct word to finish the sentences. The first one has been done as an example.

1 The woman says the food is *hot/good/delicious*.
2 The tourists' day was *fascinating/interesting/fantastic*.
3 The Palace was *interesting/tiring/beautiful*.
4 The lunch was *expensive/wonderful/delicious*.
5 The Golden Pavilion was *quiet/beautiful/good*.

LANGUAGE STUDY

Study these questions and answers in the Simple Past.

Question	Answer
How was your day?	It was fascinating.
What did you do?	In the morning we saw the Imperial Palace.
	This afternoon we went to the Daitokuji temple complex.
	Then we visited the Golden Pavilion.

Now study this table.

Simple Present	Simple Past
regular verbs	
suggest	*suggested*
recommend	*recommended*
order	*ordered*
visit	*visited*
walk	*walked*
irregular verbs	
is/are	*was / were*
do	*did*
see	*saw*
go	*went*
have	*had*
find	*found*

Work in pairs. Test each other! Cover the column on the right. Take turns choosing a verb. Can your partner remember the Simple Past form?

LISTEN AND PRACTICE

Look at these questions and answers. Check any words you don't understand in the **Word list**.

Match the questions with the correct answers. One has been done as an example.

1 Where did you go? ☐ I bought some souvenirs.
2 How did you get to the stores? ☐ I got back around 6:30.
3 What did you buy? ☐ I got there by subway.
4 How much did you spend? ☐ I had pasta.
5 What time did you get back? ☐ I ordered a beer.
6 Where did you eat? ☐ I paid about $15.
7 What did you have? ☐ Oh, I spent about $100.
8 What did you order to drink? ☒ 1 I went shopping.
9 How much did you pay? ☐ I went to a nearby restaurant.
10 What did you do after? ☐ I went to a show.
11 What did you think of it? ☐ Actually, it was awful!

Now listen and check your answers.

Listen again. Repeat the questions and answers. Check your pronunciation!

Turn to the tapescript on page 71 and work with a partner. Take turns asking and answering the questions.

WORD STUDY First, check any words you don't understand in the **Word list**. Then check (✓) the words that you can use together. The first one has been done as an example.

	food	trip	place
delicious	✓		
awful			
fantastic			
interesting			
tiring			
wonderful			

MORE PRACTICE Work in pairs. Make some more questions with *How was …?* Choose an adjective from the **Word study** to make your answer.

Example:

A *Hi, Victor! How was your trip?*
B *It was fantastic!*

How was …?

your vacation   your meal   the game
the trip   the theater   the museum

Now change partners and try again. This time, each try to add one more thing.

Example:

A *Hello, Maria. How was your vacation in Egypt?*
B *It was wonderful.*
A *What did you do?*
B *I saw the Pyramids.*

ACTIVITY

Work with a partner. Together, think of four places of interest to visit in your town or city. Also, decide on the best place to have lunch. Then read through your instructions and act out the dialog.

Student A You are a tour company representative in your town or city. Ask the tourist about his/her day.

Student B You are a tourist in your town or city. Tell the tour representative about your day.

Student A	Student B
Ask about the tourist's day. *So, how was your day?*	
	Say how it was. *It was wonderful/tiring/interesting!*
Ask what the tourist did.	
	Say two things you did in the morning.
Ask about lunchtime.	
	Say where you went for lunch and what you ate.
Ask how the food was.	
	Say how the food was.
Ask about the afternoon.	
	Say two things you did in the afternoon.

Now change roles and try the conversation again. Use different places this time.

SUMMARY

Now you can

◆ Talk about the past
   This afternoon we went to the Daitokuji temple complex.

◆ Ask someone about their day
   How was your day?

Vocabulary

around	fantastic	order (*vb*)	suggest
awful	fascinating	pasta	tiring
beautiful	find	quiet	visit
beer	get back	recommend	walk
buy	go shopping	show	wonderful
delicious	hot	spend	
dinner	interesting	souvenir	
expensive	nearby	subway	

10 Are you ready to order?

LISTENING

Listen to the dialogs in the hotel. Check (✓) the sentences you hear.

	Dialog 1	Dialog 2	Dialog 3
Do you have a reservation?	☐	☐	☐
Would you like smoking or non-smoking?	☐	☐	☐
Would you like to see the menu?	☐	☐	☐
Are you ready to order?	☐	☐	☐
Would you like anything to drink?	☐	☐	☐
Your order won't be long.	☐	☐	☐

LANGUAGE STUDY

Study this restaurant language. Check any words you don't understand in the **Word list** at the back of the book.

Waiter	Guest
Do you have a reservation?	*Yes. The name is … / No, I don't.*
Would you like smoking or non-smoking?	*Smoking/Non-smoking, please.*
Would you like to see the menu?	*Thank you.*
Are you ready to order?	*Yes, I think so.*
What would you like to start with?	*I'd like the … , please.*
as an appetizer?	*Could I have the … , please?*
Would you like anything to drink?	*Yes. A/An … , please.*
Is that everything? *Would you like anything else?*	*That's all, thank you.*
Fine. Your order won't be long.	*Thank you very much.*

Work in pairs. Test each other! Cover the column on the left. Take turns reading the guest's answers. Can your partner remember the questions?

LISTEN AND PRACTICE

Look at the menu. Check any words you don't understand in the **Word list**. Listen. What does the man order? What does the woman order? Check (✓) the things they order.

The Washington Hotel Menu

Appetizers

	man	woman
Soup of the day	☐	☐
Tomato juice	☐	☐
Melon with ham	☐	☐
Caesar salad	☐	☐

Entrées

	man	woman
Charbroiled 16 oz. steak	☐	☐
Chicken in a white wine sauce	☐	☐
Roast beef	☐	☐
Baked salmon	☐	☐

Side orders

	man	woman
Side salad	☐	☐
Green beans	☐	☐
French fries	☐	☐
Baked potato	☐	☐

Beverages

	man	woman
Mineral water	☐	☐
Orange juice	☐	☐
Soft drinks	☐	☐

House wines

	man	woman
Red	☐	☐
White	☐	☐
Rosé	☐	☐

Please ask to see our wine list and extensive dessert menu.
Service charge is NOT included.

Work in groups of three. Look at the tapescript on page 72. Practice the dialog.

MORE PRACTICE

Work in pairs. Practice taking and giving orders. Make sentences.

Example:

to start (with) / a tomato juice
A *What would you like to start with?*
B *I'd like a tomato juice, please.*

1 to start with / a tomato juice
2 as an entrée / the baked salmon
3 as an appetizer / the melon
4 to drink / a fresh orange juice
5 as an entrée / the filet
6 with that / French fries and a side salad
7 as an appetizer / the soup of the day
8 as an entrée / the chicken
9 with that / some green beans
10 to drink / a black coffee

Now work with a new partner. Choose popular food and drinks from your country to make your own examples. Make four sentences each.

Example:

A *What would you like to drink, sir?*
B *I'd like some hot sake, please.*
A *And what would you like as an appetizer?*
B *I'd like the guacamole, please.*

WORD STUDY

Put these words into the table on the following page.

beef   beer   chicken   French fries

fruit salad   ice cream   cheesecake   mineral water

pork   potatoes   red wine   green beans

Meat	Vegetable	Dessert	Drink
_____	_____	_____	_____
_____	_____	_____	_____
_____	_____	_____	_____

Can you think of some more words to add to each column?

ACTIVITY

Work in small groups. Look at the menu on page 41. Take turns being the waiter/waitress and guests.

Guests: Look at the menu and decide what you would like to eat and drink.
Waitress/waiter: Take the guests' orders.

(Look at the **Language study** again on page 40 if you need help.)

When you have finished, change roles and try again.

SUMMARY

Now you can
- Greet restaurant guests
  Do you have a reservation?
- Take orders
  What would you like to start with?
- Understand orders
  I'd like the green salad, please.

Vocabulary

appetizer	fresh orange juice	roast beef
baked potato	green beans	side order
baked salmon	charbroiled 16 oz. steak	side salad
beverage	house wine	soft drink
Caesar salad	meat	soup of the day
chicken in a white wine sauce	melon with ham	tomato juice
dessert	menu	vegetable
entrée	mineral water	
French fries	order (*n*)	

How will you be paying?

LISTENING

Listen to three dialogs. Decide if these sentences are true (T) or false (F).

1   a   ☐ The bag costs $45 including tax.
    b   ☐ The customer pays by credit card.

2   a   ☐ The customer is changing ten thousand yen into Hong Kong dollars.
    b   ☐ The customer gets $88.88.

3   a   ☐ The check is for $10.70 including tax.
    b   ☐ The customer pays by traveler's check.

LANGUAGE STUDY

Study these questions and answers.

Clerk	Customer
Can I help you?	*Yes, please. How much is this ......?*
	are these ... ?
How would you like to pay?	*Can I pay cash?*
	Can I pay by (traveler's) check?
	Can I pay by credit card?
	Do you accept credit cards?
Could I have your card, please?	*Yes, here you are.*
Can I help you?	*Yes, please. I'd like to change some money.*
How much would you like to change?	*I'd like to change ... into ... , please.*
We charge two percent (2%) commission.	*That's fine.*
That comes to ...	*Fine.*

Work in pairs. Test each other! Cover the column on the left and take turns reading what the customer says. Can your partner remember what the clerk says?

Look at how we say prices.

It's $10.50
It's ten dollars and fifty cents.
It's ten fifty.

I'd like to change ¥10,000 ...
I'd like to change ten thousand yen ...

LISTEN AND PRACTICE

Write the following sentences in the correct order to make two dialogs. The first sentence of each dialog has been done as an example.

OK, I'll take one.
Certainly, ma'am. How much would you like to change?
All right ... That comes to nine thousand, one hundred yen.
How would you like to pay?
They're eighteen fifty.
Do you accept credit cards?
Here you are.
OK. We charge two percent commission.
How much are these books?
Two percent? That's fine.
I'd like to change one hundred US dollars into yen, please.
Yes, sir. Could I have your card, please?
I'd like to change some money.

Dialog 1

1 *How much are these books?*
2 _____
3 _____
4 _____
5 _____
6 _____
7 _____

Dialog 2

a *I'd like to change some money.*
b _____
c _____
d _____
e _____
f _____

Listen to the dialogs and check your answers.

Then work with a partner. Practice the dialogs.

MORE PRACTICE

Work with a partner. Choose dialog **1** or **2** below and practice it with a partner.

1

Customer
- How much is this book?
- OK, I'll take it.
- Do you accept credit cards?
- OK.

Clerk
- It's fourteen dollars and fifty cents.
- How would you like to pay?
- I'm sorry, sir. We only accept cash.

Now make a similar conversation using these cues. Try not to look at the dialog above.

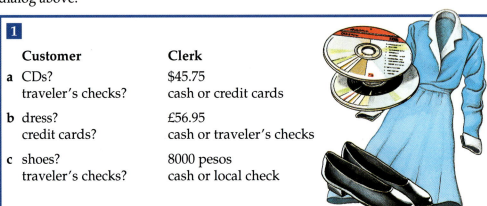

1

	Customer	Clerk
a	CDs? traveler's checks?	$45.75 cash or credit cards
b	dress? credit cards?	£56.95 cash or traveler's checks
c	shoes? traveler's checks?	8000 pesos cash or local check

2

Customer
- I'd like to change some yen.
- I'd like to change two thousand yen into US dollars, please.
- That's fine.
- OK.

Clerk
- Certainly, ma'am. How much would you like to change?
- OK. We charge 2 percent commission.
- All right ... That comes to $180.

Now make a similar conversation using these cues. Try not to look at the dialog on the opposite page.

2

	Customer	Clerk
a	pesos 1500 pesos/pounds	how much? 1 ½%
b	won 60 000 won/A$	how much? 1 ½%
c	baht 3500 baht/US$	how much? 2 ½%

ACTIVITY Work in pairs or groups. Complete the table below using these words.

baht   MXN   dollars   pesos
dollars   South Korea   Hong Kong   Thailand
Japan   THB   USD   JPY
KRW   won   Mexico

Country	Currency	Currency abbreviation used by banks
_____	_____	_____
USA	_____	_____
_____	_____	_____
_____	yen	_____
_____	_____	HKD
_____	_____	_____

SUMMARY

Now you can

◆ Talk about money
That's about 80 dollars.

◆ Ask about payment
How will you be paying?

◆ Change money for someone
How much would you like to change?

Vocabulary

accept	check (*n*)	currency	pay
change money	commission	including tax	percent
charge (*vb*)	cost	(local) check	That comes to ...

12 We'll meet back here at three o'clock

LISTENING

Listen to the guide. Complete the notes on the itinerary. Choose the correct answer. The first one has been done as an example.

South Peruvian tour itinerary

Tuesday
7:00	Leave Lima by *train/<u>bus</u>/plane*
12:00	Have *coffee/picnic/lunch* at Pisco at the hotel
13:00	Take *boat/plane* to Ballestas Islands
17:00	Bus to *Nazca/Las Dunas*
Evening	*Drinks/Dinner/Party* at hotel

Wednesday
6:00	*Get up/Have breakfast*
6:30	Take *bus/taxi* to airport
7:00	Take *plane/helicopter* to see the Nazca Lines

LANGUAGE STUDY

Study this language.

In a few minutes, we'll leave Lima.
At one o'clock, we'll take a boat to the islands.
We'll drive to the hotel for dinner.
We won't land on the islands, but we will have drinks and snacks on the boat.
How long will we stay in Nazca?

Work with a partner. Practice reading the sentences.

When we describe an itinerary, we often use these phrases.

First, ...	*Then ...*	*After lunch, ...*	*Later, ...*
Next, ...	*After that, ...*	*At three o'clock, ...*	*Finally, ...*

Now work with a partner. Talk about the itinerary in the **Listening**. Take turns.
Example:
First, we'll leave Lima by bus at 7 o'clock.
At 12 o'clock, we'll .....
Then ...

LISTEN AND PRACTICE

Listen to the cassette and fill in the blanks.

1 _____ here for 10 minutes. Please be back at the bus _____ 11:30.

2 Please _____ to take all your belongings with you.

3 You are _____ to take photographs outside, but please do not use a flash inside the palace.

4 I have your group entry ticket. Please keep together until we are _____ .

5 The afternoon is _____ . The bus _____ again at 5:30 p.m.

6 _____ stop in front of the palace so that _____ take photographs.

7 We'll _____ here for one hour to give you a chance to _____ and buy souvenirs.

8 _____ back here at 3 o'clock.

Listen again and repeat the announcements. Practice your pronunciation!

49

MORE PRACTICE

Match the questions to the answers. The first one has been done as an example.

1 How long will we stay here?
2 Will we have a guided tour?
3 Where are we staying tonight?
4 Where can I buy souvenirs?
5 Do I have time to climb to the top?
6 Can we take photographs?
7 Would you take a photo of us, please?
8 Where can I get a cold drink?

☐ No, I'm afraid you don't. We'll only be here for ten minutes.
☐ There are some good stores in the market behind the hotel.
☐ Yes, but please don't use a flash.
☐ There's a bar over there.
[1] About 45 minutes. Please return to the bus by 10:30.
☐ Yes. The guide will meet us at the entrance.
☐ Certainly. Ready? Say "Cheese!"
☐ At the Florida Hotel in the city center.

Work with a partner. Take turns asking and answering the questions. Practice your pronunciation.

ACTIVITY

You are the guide for Day 6 and Day 7 of the *China Tour*. Here is their itinerary. Work with a partner. Follow the instructions on the opposite page to help you talk through the itinerary. (Look back at the **Language study** if you need help). Take turns giving the whole speech.

China Tour excursion

Xian tour itinerary

Day 6

15:00 Transfer from the hotel to the airport for a flight to Xian.

Stay overnight at the Bell Tower Hotel, Xian.

Day 7

07:30 Take the bus to the emperor's burial mound. See the terracotta warriors.

12:00 Return to the bus. Have lunch in Ban Po.

13:30 Take the tour of the ancient village at Ban Po.

15:30 Return to the coach. Visit the hot springs at Huaqing.

17:00 Return to Xian.

Evening: See the Tang Dynasty Dance Show.

Have dinner and stay overnight at the hotel.

1 Greet the tourists.
Good morning, ...

2 Introduce yourself.
My name is ... I'm your guide for the next two days.

3 Say you are going to tell everyone the itinerary for the next 2 days.

4 Talk through Days 6 and 7.
First ... Then ...

5 Ask if there are any questions.

6 Tell the tourists to enjoy themselves!

Work in pairs or small groups. Plan an itinerary for a group of tourists visiting your area. Then join another group and take turns announcing your itineraries. Use as much English as you can.

Example:

Good afternoon, everyone. It's a lovely day today for our trip to the castle and old town. My name is ... etc.

SUMMARY

Now you can

- Explain plans and itineraries to a tour group
  First, we'll leave Lima by bus at 7 o'clock.

- Answer common questions asked by tourists
  Where can I buy souvenirs?
  There are some good stores in the market.

Vocabulary

ancient	hot springs	snack
belongings	inside	stay
boat	island	stay overnight
climb	itinerary	stop
drive	keep together	tonight
flash	land (*vb*)	top
free	look around	transfer
get up	market	use
give you a chance to	meet (2)	village
group entry ticket	over there	you are welcome to ...
guided tour	picnic	
helicopter	remember	

13 Why don't you take the city bus tour?

LISTENING

An American tourist is in a tourist information office in Mexico City. He is asking about what to do and see in Mexico. Listen to the dialog. Check (✓) the places the information officer suggests.

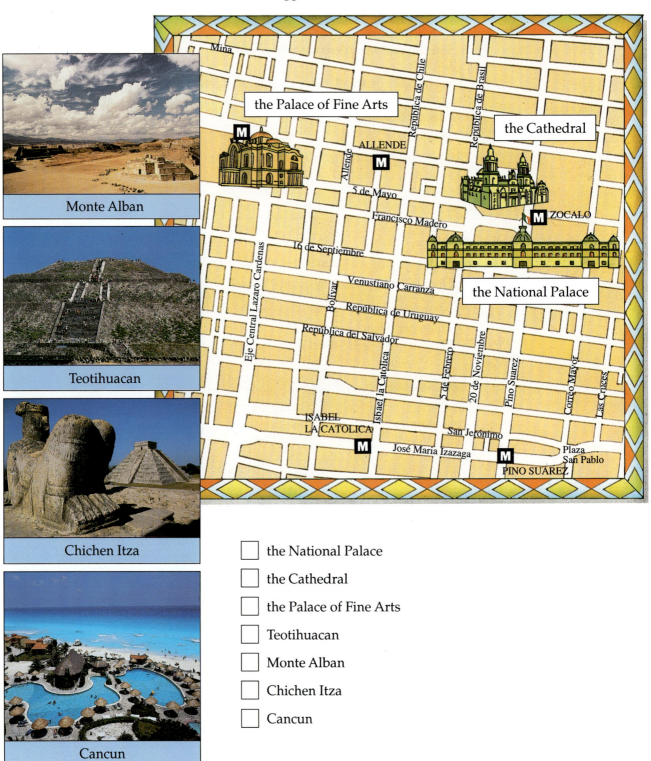

- [ ] the National Palace
- [ ] the Cathedral
- [ ] the Palace of Fine Arts
- [ ] Teotihuacan
- [ ] Monte Alban
- [ ] Chichen Itza
- [ ] Cancun

LANGUAGE STUDY

Study these sentences.

> *Why don't you take a city bus tour?*
> *I suggest you take a day trip to the beach.*
> *I think you should also visit the museum.*
> *You could visit Chichen Itza.*

Read the suggestions aloud. Practice your pronunciation!

Study these adjectives and nouns.

Adjective	Noun
main	tourist attractions
ancient	city
beautiful	beaches
important	historical sites
excellent	map
wonderful	day trip

Check any words you don't understand in the **Word list**.

LISTEN AND PRACTICE

Listen and match the phrases. The first one has been done as an example.

1. Why don't you fly there ...
2. I suggest you stay overnight ...
3. I recommend you visit ...
4. You could take the train one way ...
5. Why don't you visit the shrines first ...
6. Are you interested in ...
7. I strongly recommend a railpass ...
8. I suggest you visit the Palace this morning while it's cool, ...

- [ ] ... and fly back.
- [ ] ... and then go to the shopping mall?
- [ ] ... and visit the art gallery in the afternoon.
- [ ] ... because it's a very good deal.
- [ ] ... in one of the temple guesthouses.
- [ ] ... one of the traditional villages.
- [1] ... to save time?
- [ ] ... walking tours?

Practice making the suggestions.

MORE PRACTICE

Choose the correct adjectives to fill in the blanks. The first one has been done as an example.

1. The *ancient* pyramids at Teotihuacan are an important tourist attraction. (ancient/traditional)
2. The _____ western greeting is a handshake. (traditional/old)
3. There are many fine restaurants serving _____ food. (delicious/beautiful)
4. It's a _____ city full of nightclubs and bars. (peaceful/lively)
5. On weekends the beaches are always very _____ . (crowded/famous)
6. One of the most _____ temples in Kyoto is the Golden Pavilion. (famous/main)
7. People who want a _____ holiday often go to the mountains. (comfortable/quiet)
8. The hotel has a fine restaurant with _____ service. (excellent/important)
9. The Great Barrier Reef is a _____ place for scuba diving. (delicious/wonderful)
10. Sunrise over Ayers Rock is a _____ sight. (strong/fantastic)

ACTIVITY

In pairs, take turns being a tourist and a tourist information officer. The tourist reads one of the sentences aloud, and asks *What do you recommend/suggest?* The tourist information officer recommends one of the places in the pictures. Use all the pictures.

Example:

A *I'm interested in nightlife. What do you suggest?*
B *Well, why don't you go the "Starlight" dance club? They play great music!*
A *That's a good idea. Thanks!*

I like lively, crowded places.
I just want to relax.
I want excellent service.
I like peaceful places.
I want to be near the beach.
I want to go somewhere cool.
I'm here to see some ancient ruins.
I'm interested in night-life.

the Hotel Tara · the Black Mountains · the Palm Hotel
the City Art Gallery · Lake Peaceful · the Golden Temple
the ancient city of Anca · the San Isidro market · the "Starlight" dance club

Now try again. This time, recommend places in your area.

SUMMARY

Now you can

- Make suggestions and recommendations
  Why don't you take the city bus tour?
- Describe tourist attractions
  Teotihuacan is an important historical site.

Vocabulary

attraction	full of	nightclub	scuba diving	walking tour
beach	good deal	over	shrine	weekend
comfortable	greeting	palace	sight	
cool	guesthouse	peaceful	site	
crowded	handshake	place	strongly	
excellent	historical	pyramid	sunrise	
famous	important	railpass	relax	
fine	lively	ruins	temple	
fly	mountain	save time	traditional	

14 Shall I send you a brochure?

LISTENING

Someone is calling a travel agency to get information about a vacation. First, read the sentences below. Then listen to the dialog. Are the sentences true (T) or false (F)?

1 The caller wants to know about the vacation special to Thailand and Malaysia.
2 There is a discount for groups of ten people or more.
3 The caller doesn't want a brochure.
4 There are ten places left on the tour leaving on January 8th.
5 The travel clerk will hold the places on the tour until next Thursday.

LANGUAGE STUDY

Study these offers.

Travel Agent	Customer
Shall I send you a brochure?	*Yes, please.*
I'll mail you the brochure today.	*Thank you.*
Would you like me to hold those places?	*That would be great.*

Work in pairs. Test each other! Cover the column on the left. Take turns reading the answers aloud. Can your partner remember the offer?

LISTEN AND PRACTICE

Listen to these dialogs in a travel agency. Fill in the blanks.

Dialog 1

A Do you have any information about vacation tours in Chile?

B Yes, we do. _____ send you some brochures?

A Yes, please.

B Could _____ your name and address?

Dialog 2

A I'd like to speak to Mr. De Vito.

B I'm afraid he's in a meeting. _____ take a message?

A No, that's OK, thanks. I'll call back later.

Dialog 3

A I'm sorry, I lost my itinerary.

B Don't worry. _____ send you a copy.

A That would be great.

Dialog 4

A _____ nights is it for?

B It's for 3 nights, from the 12th through the 14th of August.

A I see. Just a moment, please, and _____ check for you.

Listen again and repeat the dialogs. Check your pronunciation.

Work with a partner. Take turns being the travel agent. Practice each dialog twice.

MORE PRACTICE

Match the tourist's problem with an offer of help. The first one has been done for you.

1 Do you have a double room for tonight?
2 I've lost my luggage tags.
3 Could you tell me where the museum is, please?
4 I feel sick.
5 Someone took my wallet. It has all my credit cards.
6 I left my watch at the swimming pool.
7 I'm cold.
8 Could we pay, please?
9 What time does the Science Museum open?
10 These bags are really heavy!

☐ Don't worry. I'll get you some more.
☐ I'll call the swimming pool attendant to see if he found it.
☐ I'll carry them for you.
☒ 1 I'll just check availability for you.
☐ I'll show you where it is on the map.
☐ I'm not sure. Would you like me to call them and find out for you?
☐ Should I call a doctor?
☐ Should I get you a blanket?
☐ Sure. I'll get your check.
☐ Would you like me to call the police?

Now work in pairs. Practice the dialogs. Take turns being the tourist.

ACTIVITY

Play this game in groups. Throw a dice and move around the board. If you land on a situation, you must offer to help using *Should I ... ?*, *I'll ...* , or *Would you like me to ... ?* Use the cues in parentheses to help you.

Example:
You work as a bellhop. You see a guest carrying two large bags. (carry)
I'll carry those for you.

If you make a mistake, miss a turn.

The first person to land on *Finish* is the winner!

SUMMARY

Now you can

- Offer to help people
  Would you like me to send you a brochure?

- Understand and deal with tourists' problems
  *I feel sick.
  Should I call a doctor?*

Vocabulary

availability	copy	later	place (2)	wallet
be left	discount	lost	police	watch
blanket	doctor	mail	really	
brochure	Don't worry.	meeting	science	
carry	feel sick	more	send	
cathedral	great	museum	someone	
check (*vb*)	heavy	next	tomorrow	
cold	interested in	painkiller	vacation special	

15 I look forward to hearing from you

LISTENING

Eva is from Brazil. She is having an interview in English for a job in a travel agency. First, look at the sentences below. Then listen to the job interview and choose the correct answers. The first one has been done for you.

1 Eva was born in *São Paulo/<u>Rio de Janeiro</u>/the United States*.
2 She has visited *Canada/the United States/Australia*.
3 She went there *last summer/last winter/two months ago*.
4 Eva's favorite subject was *English/tourism/business administration*.
5 Eva took the TOEFL examination *in high school/one year ago/one month ago*.

LANGUAGE STUDY

We use has/have done (the Present Perfect) to talk about experiences, when we do not know or want to know when something happened.

Have you always lived in Brazil?	*Yes, I have.*
Have you taken any English exams?	*Yes, I have.*
Have you ever worked in a travel agency?	*No, I haven't.*

If we know or want to know <u>when</u> something happened, we use the Simple Past.

When did you go to the USA?	*I went last summer.*
When did you take the TOEIC exam?	*I took it last month.*

LISTEN AND PRACTICE

Kyoko Tanaka

Address	Zenpukuji 2-26-4 Suginami-ku Tokyo 168
Telephone number	03 6486 7741
Nationality	Japanese

Education and training

1990-94	Koganei-kita High School, Tokyo
1994-96	Tokyo Air Travel College Subjects include word processing, business administration, and English.

Other information

Typing	70 wpm
Languages	Japanese, intermediate English
Interests	Reading and tennis
	References to be supplied upon request.

Put the following sentences in the correct order to make a conversation between Kyoko and her interviewer. The first one has been done as an example.

☐ Oh really? How fast can you type?

☐ Yes, I'm Kyoko Tanaka.

☐ Well, my name is Kyoko and I'm 19 years old. I'm studying at Tokyo Air Travel College and I'll graduate next March. I hope to work in the travel industry next year.

☐ Have you taken any exams in English?

[1] Good morning. Please take a seat. Can I have your name, please?

☐ 70 words a minute.

☐ Thank you, Ms. Tanaka. Could you tell me a little bit about yourself?

☐ Thank you.

☐ Yes, I took the TOEIC exam last month. But I've also taken exams in word processing and business administration.

☐ That's very fast! Well, thank you, Ms. Tanaka. Please wait here while I ask Mr. Takahashi, our personnel manager, to come in and see you.

☐ Good. Which languages can you speak?

☐ I speak Japanese and some English.

Now listen and check your answers.

Listen again and repeat the conversation. Check your pronunciation!

Work with a partner. Turn to the tapescript on page 77 and practice the conversation.

61

MORE PRACTICE

Look at these interview questions and answers. Check any words you don't understand in the **Word list** at the back of the book.

Question	Answer
1 Could I have your name, please?	Yes, my name is ...
2 How old are you?	I'm ... years old.
3 Where are you from?	I'm from ...
4 What do you do?	I'm a student.
5 Where do you study?	I study at ... (school name).
6 Which languages do you speak?	I speak ...
7 Have you taken any English exams?	No, I haven't. / Yes, I have. I took ... (exam name) in ... (year).
8 What are your interests?	Well, I really enjoy ... (your hobbies).
9 Do you have any work experience?	No, I don't. / Yes, I do. I work part-time in a ...
10 Have you ever traveled overseas?	No, I haven't. But I would like to go to ... / Yes, I have. I went to ... (place) in ... (year).

Now work in pairs. Take turns being Younghee and Eduardo. Interview each other using the questions above and the information about Younghee and Eduardo.

Personal history

Name	Younghee Kim	**Age**	20
Nationality	South Korean	**Occupation**	Student
Name of school	Central Tourism College		
Languages	Korean, some English		
English exams taken	TOEFL (last year)		
Interests	Reading, playing volleyball		
Work experience	None		
Travel	Never traveled abroad		

Personal history

Name	Eduardo Mendoza	**Age**	21
Nationality	Mexican	**Occupation**	Student
Name of school	Benito Juárez College		
Languages	Spanish and English		
English exams taken	None		
Interests	Playing baseball		
Work experience	Work in a restaurant on weekends		
Travel	USA (last year)		

ACTIVITY Work in pairs. Complete the form about your partner by asking him or her questions. Check any words you don't understand in the **Word list**.

Personal history

Name _____ Age _____

Nationality _____

Occupation _____

Name of school _____

Languages _____

English exams taken _____

Interests _____

Work experience _____

Travel _____

SUMMARY Now you can

♦ Talk about experiences

Have you ever worked in a travel agency?
Yes, I have.

♦ Ask and answer interview questions

Do you have any work experience?
No, I don't.

Vocabulary

ago	graduate	overseas
always	high school	personnel manager
be born	hope	summer
business administration	industry	tourism
ever	interview	training
exam	language	type
examination	last	winter
experience	month	word processing
fast	nationality	year
favorite	occupation	

Tapescripts

1

LISTENING Listen to four dialogs. Write the dialog number next to the correct picture.

Dialog 1
A Good morning. I'm Akira Kambara.
B I'm Chris Bailey. Pleased to meet you, Mr. Kambara.
A Pleased to meet you, Mr. Bailey.

Dialog 2
A Excuse me. Are you Mrs. Lee?
B Yes, that's right.
A Hello, my name's Eduardo Vargas.
B Pleased to meet you.

Dialog 3
A Hello, everyone! It's nice to meet you! Welcome to Bangkok!

Dialog 4
A Good evening, Mrs. Parker.
B Good evening.

LISTEN AND PRACTICE Judy Wong is a tour company representative. She is meeting a tour group. Listen to the dialog.

Man Excuse me. Are you the Sunrise tour rep?
Judy Yes, I am. Excuse me! Could you listen for a moment? ...
Thank you. Good morning, everybody. I'd like to introduce myself. My name is Judy Wong and I'm from Taipei. I'm the tour rep for East-West Tours. It's very nice to meet you all. Welcome to Taiwan. Now, is everybody here ...?

2

LISTENING Listen to five dialogs about jobs. Write the dialog number next to the correct picture.

Dialog 1
A So, what do you do, Monica?
B I'm a hotel receptionist.
A Oh, yeah? Where do you work?
B At the Waldorf.

Dialog 2
A Excuse me! Are you a waiter? I'd like another cup of coffee.
B Actually, I'm not a waiter, sir, I'm a bartender. But I'll have a waiter come to your table.
A Thank you.

Dialog 3
A Does he work in New York?
B No, he doesn't. He works in Washington, D.C.
A What exactly does he do?
B He works for a big travel agency. He's a travel clerk.

64

Dialog 4
A Do they work in a hotel?
B No, they don't. They work for Japan Airlines.
A Are they flight attendants?
B Yes, they are.

Dialog 5
A What do you do?
B I'm a tour representative with Jasmine Tours.
A Oh, yeah? Where do you work?
B In Chiang Mai. You know, Northern Thailand.

LISTEN AND PRACTICE

Listen to the dialogs and complete the sentences.

Dialog 1
A What do you do?
B I'm a tour guide.

Dialog 2
A Is he a bellhop?
B No, he isn't. He's a receptionist.

Dialog 3
A Where do you work?
B In a hotel. I'm a waiter.

Dialog 4
A Are you a travel clerk?
B Yes, I am. I work in New York.

Dialog 5
A Do you work in a hotel?
B No, I don't. I work in a tourist information office.

3

LISTENING

Write down the time you hear.

Dialog 1
A Thank you, Mr. Ramos. Your flight leaves from Terminal 3. Please check in at ten fifteen at counter B.
B Ten fifteen? I see. Thank you very much.

Dialog 2
A Can you help me? What time is the first bus to Pattaya?
B Just a moment ... The bus leaves at seven in the morning.
A 7 o'clock? Thanks.

Dialog 3
A I need to change some money. Are the banks still open?
B Actually, they close at three thirty so you'd better hurry!
A Three thirty? You're joking! I'd better run!

Dialog 4
A That's all, Dr. Nelson. Is there anything else you'd like?
B Um ... I don't think so. Oh yes, what time is lunch?
A Lunch is served from eleven forty-five in the main restaurant.
B Eleven forty-five. That's fine. Thank you.
A Thank you, ma'am.

Dialog 5
A Thank you, everybody. That's all. Now, are there any questions?
B Yes. Can we go shopping now?
A Yes, of course. We'll meet back here at six fifty. That's six fifty, and please don't be late!

Dialog 6
A Excuse me. What time is the National Park open to visitors?
B It opens at nine fifteen every day.
A I see. Thank you.

LISTEN AND PRACTICE

Listen to the cassette. Match the pictures, verbs, and times. Draw a line.

1 The train leaves at seven forty-five in the morning.
2 The bank closes at half past three in the afternoon.
3 The department store opens at nine a.m.
4 Breakfast is served from seven thirty a.m.
5 The bus arrives at a quarter after five in the evening.

4

LISTENING

Listen to three dialogs. For each dialog, check the card (a or b) with the correct information.

Dialog 1
A Edgware Inn. Can I help you?
B Yes. I'd like to reserve a single room, please.
A Certainly, sir. What's your name, please?
B Baughan, that's B-A-U-G-H-A-N.
A Thank you, Mr. Baughan. When will you be arriving?
B April 1st.
A For how many nights?
B Until April 6th.
A So that's a single room for five nights.

Dialog 2
A What kind of room would you like, Ms. Chang?
B A single room with bath, please.
A I'm sorry. I can only offer you a single with shower or a double with bath.
A I'll take the double room with bath, then.

Dialog 3
A OK, Mr. Stephens. I can confirm your reservation. Now, how will you be paying?
B By traveler's check.
A I'm sorry, we don't accept traveler's checks. We take credit cards or cash.
B I see. I'll pay by credit card then, I guess. Visa.
A Thank you, sir. What's the card number, please?
B It's 1234 567 890.

LISTEN AND PRACTICE Listen to the dialog and check your answers.

A I'd like to make a reservation, please.
B Certainly, sir. What's your name, please?
A Williamson, Bill Williamson.
B When will you be arriving, Mr. Williamson?
A July 12th.
B For how many nights?
A Until the 14th.
B So that's two nights.
A Yes, two nights.
B And what kind of room would you like?
A A single room with bath, please.
B And how will you be paying, Mr. Williamson?
A By Visa.
B That's fine. What's the card number, please?
A It's 0123 456 7890.
B And what's your address, please?
A It's 1738 Lincoln Drive, Washington, D.C. 26676.
B OK, Mr. Williamson, I can confirm your reservation. That's a single room for two nights from July 12th.
A Thank you.

5

LISTENING Listen to the cassette. What are they talking about? Write the dialog number next to the correct picture.

Dialog 1
A Excuse me. Can I leave my bag on the bus?
B No, I'm afraid not. Could you all listen, please? Don't leave your bags on the bus. It's not safe. Take everything with you.

Dialog 2
A Do you have a name tag on that bag?
B Oh no, I don't.
A OK. Write your name and address on this tag, please.
B Do you have a pen?
A Certainly. Here you are.

Dialog 3
A Thank you, Mr. Garcia. Your flight is confirmed.
B Thank you.
A Please check in at least two hours before your flight.
B I see. Thank you very much.

Dialog 4
A Passengers on flight KE 907, please have your boarding pass ready. Passengers on flight KE 907, please have your boarding pass ready. Thank you.

Dialog 5
A Please go through Immigration now. Have your passport and visa ready.
B I'm sorry, what did she say?
C We're going through Immigration. Have your passport and visa ready.

LISTEN AND PRACTICE

Listen and complete these instructions.

1 Don't leave your bags on the tour bus.
2 Write your name and address on this tag, please.
3 Please check in at least two hours before your flight.
4 Have your boarding pass ready.
5 Please go immediately to gate 37.
6 Do not leave any bags unattended.
7 Please board the plane through door E.
8 Fasten your seatbelt.
9 Do not smoke until you are inside the terminal building.
10 Enjoy your flight!

LISTENING

Listen. Where is each place? Draw a line to the correct floor in the hotel.

Dialog 1
Guest Excuse me. Where's the restaurant, please?
Clerk It's on the second floor, sir. The stairs are over there on the left, or there's an elevator on the right.
G Thank you.

Dialog 2
G Is there somewhere I can park my car?
C Yes, ma'am. There's a parking lot for guests in the basement. The entrance is behind the hotel.
G Thank you.
C Thank you, ma'am.

Dialog 3
G Excuse me. Is the cocktail bar on the first floor? Only I can't seem to find it.
C No, sir. The cocktail bar is on the third floor.
G I see. Thank you.

Dialog 4
G I'm looking for the lounge.
C It's next to the swimming pool on the second floor.
G Next to the swimming pool on the second floor. Thank you.

Dialog 5
G Is there a telephone I can use?
C Yes, sir. There are some telephones on the first floor near the main entrance.

Dialog 6
G Can I change some money here?
C We have an exchange bureau, but it's closed until 10 a.m.
G OK. Where exactly is it?
C It's upstairs on the second floor.

LISTEN AND PRACTICE

Listen to the information clerk in the shopping mall telling people where things are. Where are these places?

1 the car rental office
2 the drugstore
3 the bus stop
4 the pizza parlor
5 the lost and found office

Listen and write a number on the plan.

1   A Excuse me. Where can I rent a car?
    B Go straight through the mall, past the fountain. The car rental office is in the corner on the right, next to the sandwich bar.
    A In the corner on the right ... Thanks!

2   A Can you help me? I'm looking for the drugstore.
    B Yes, of course. It's upstairs, on the second floor, next to the post office. It's across from the bank.
    A Thank you so much.

3   A Excuse me. Where do I take the city bus tour from?
    B The bus stop is just around the corner. Leave by the main entrance here. Turn right. Then take the second right. The bus stop is next to the park.
    A I see. I turn right at the main entrance, take the second right, and it's next to the park.
    B That's it.
    A Thanks a lot.

4   A Excuse me. Where's the pizza parlor?
    B It's upstairs on the third floor, between the travel agency and the bookstore.
    A On the third floor?
    B Yes, that's right.

5   A Excuse me, please. Is there a lost and found office in the mall?
    B Yes. Take the elevator to the second floor and turn left. Go past the art gallery on your left. Take the second right, and it's on your right. It's next to the travel center.

7

LISTENING

Listen to the telephone conversation and fill in the blanks.

A Good morning, Oriental Hotel, Bangkok. Can I help you?
B Hello. Could I speak to the General Manager, please?
A I'm afraid he's not here at the moment. Can I take a message?
B Yes, please. My name is Mr. Lopez, Roberto Lopez. Could you ask him to call me after 3 p.m. today?
A Certainly, Mr. Lopez. Could I have your number?
B Yes, it's 247 1033.
A Thank you. I'll give him the message.

LISTEN AND PRACTICE

Listen and check your answers.

R Good afternoon. Minata House. How may I help you?
C Could I speak to Mrs. Chang, please?
R I'm sorry. Mrs. Chang isn't here at the moment.
C Do you know what time she'll be back?
R I think she'll be back this afternoon. Can I take a message?
C Yes, please. Could you ask her to call me? My name is Mr. Jackson.
R Certainly, sir. Could you spell that, please?
C It's J-A-C-K-S-O-N. I'm staying at the Renada Hotel.
R The Renada Hotel? Could I have your number?
C Yes, it's 43 66 21.
R Thank you very much, Mr. Jackson. I'll give her the message.
C Thank you. Goodbye.
R Goodbye.

8

LISTENING

Listen to the dialog and check your answers.

Check-in clerk Good morning. May I see your passport and ticket, please?
Passenger Sure. Here you are.
C Thank you, sir ... Could you put your baggage on the scales, please, Mr. Sampras?
P OK.
C Just the two pieces?
P Yes, just two.
C That's fine. Do you have any hand luggage?
P Yes, this small bag.
C That's fine. Would you fill out this name tag and attach it to your bag, please?
P Sure. Do you have a pen?
C Here you are.
P Thanks.
C Would you like a window seat or an aisle seat?
P A window seat, please.
C All right, Mr. Sampras ... Can you go straight through to the Departure Lounge now, please. The flight is boarding now.
P Fine. Thanks a lot.
C You're welcome. Enjoy your flight.

LISTEN AND PRACTICE

Listen to these conversations in a tourist information office. Fill in the blanks.

Dialog 1
Clerk Good morning. Can I help you?
Tourist Yes, please. I'd like to reserve two seats on the city tour today.
C Yes, certainly. May I have your name?

Dialog 2
C Good morning. May I help you?
T Can we leave our luggage here for 24 hours?
C Yes, you can. Would you fill out this form, please?
T Sure. Do you have a pen, please?

Dialog 3

C May I help you?
T Yes, please. I'd like to change some traveler's checks.
C Certainly. May I have some ID, please?
T I have my driver's license.
C That's fine.

Dialog 4

T Excuse me. Can you help me with accommodations?
C Certainly, madam. Could you please just wait until I finish helping this gentleman?
T No problem.

9

LISTENING

Listen to the conversation. What do they say? Choose the correct word to finish the sentences.

Man This is a lovely restaurant, Mayumi.
Mayumi This is one of the best tempura restaurants in Kyoto.
Woman The food really is delicious.
Man Would you like something to drink, Mayumi? Perhaps some hot sake or Japanese green tea?
Mayumi Green tea would be wonderful.
Woman Sake for me.
Mayumi So, how was your day?
Woman Oh, very good. It was fascinating.
Mayumi What did you do?
Woman In the morning, we saw the Imperial Palace. It was very interesting.
Man Then, this afternoon, we went to the Daitokuji temple complex. We had a wonderful lunch at the Zen restaurant.
Mayumi Oh good! You found it.
Woman Then we visited the Golden Pavilion – it's so beautiful, and then we walked around the Zen garden on the grounds of the Ryoanji temple.
Mayumi Oh yes, it really is a wonderful place.

LISTEN AND PRACTICE

Listen and check your answers.

1 Where did you go?
   I went shopping.
2 How did you get to the stores?
   I got there by subway.
3 What did you buy?
   I bought some souvenirs.
4 How much did you spend?
   Oh, I spent about $100.
5 What time did you get back?
   I got back around 6:30.
6 Where did you eat?
   I went to a nearby restaurant.
7 What did you have?
   I had pasta.
8 What did you order to drink?
   I ordered a beer.

9 How much did you pay?
I paid about $15.
10 What did you do after?
I went to a show.
11 What did you think of it?
Actually, it was awful!

10

LISTENING

Listen to the dialogs in the hotel. Check the sentences you hear.

Dialog 1
A Do you have a reservation, sir?
B Yes. My name is Howard.
A ... Yes, sir. A table for four. Would you like smoking or non-smoking?
B Non-smoking, please.
A Fine, sir. Would you follow me, please?

Dialog 2
A Are you ready to order?
B Yes, I'd like the pâté to start.
A One pâté.
B And I'd like a pepperoni pizza and a salad to follow, please.
A ... Pepperoni pizza and salad ... Would you like anything to drink?
B An orange juice, please.
A Certainly. Your order won't be long ...

Dialog 3
A Would you like to see the menu?
B Yes, please.
...
I think we're ready to order. Could we have number sixteen for two, please?
A That's fine. Would you like anything to drink?
B Beer for me.
C I'll take a beer also.
A Is that everything?
B Yes, thank you.

LISTEN AND PRACTICE

Listen. What does the man order? What does the woman order? Check the things they order.

Waiter Good afternoon. Do you have a reservation?
Man Yes, we do. My name is Brayton.
Waiter Yes, sir. A table for two?
Man That's right.
Waiter Would you like smoking or non-smoking?
Woman Non-smoking, please.
...
Waiter Are you ready to order?
Man Yes, we are.
Waiter What would you like to start with?
Woman I'd like the melon, please.
Waiter One melon. And for you, sir?
Man What exactly is the soup of the day?
Waiter It's gazpacho, sir. Basically it's cold tomato soup.

Man Cold soup? Oh ... maybe not ... I'll have the Caesar salad, please.
Waiter Certainly, sir. And as an entrée?
Woman I'd like the baked salmon, please.
Waiter Any side orders with that?
Woman Yes. A side salad, I guess.
Waiter One salmon and one side salad. OK. And for you, sir?
Man I'd like the roast beef, please.
Waiter Yes, sir. What would you like with that?
Man Ah ... I'll take an order of green beans and a baked potato, please.
Waiter Certainly, sir. And what would you like to drink?
Man What would you like, honey?
Woman I'll have a glass of white wine, please.
Man And could I have an iced mineral water, please?
Waiter Certainly, sir. Is that everything?
Man That's all, thank you.
Waiter Thank you, sir ... madam. Your order won't be long.

11

LISTENING Listen to three dialogs. Decide if these sentences are true or false.

Dialog 1
A Can I help you?
B Yes, please. How much is this bag?
A It's forty-five dollars with tax.
B OK, I'll take it.
A How would you like to pay?
B Can I pay cash? No, wait a moment, do you accept credit cards? I don't think I have enough cash.
A That's fine. Could I have your card, please?
B Sure. Here you are.

Dialog 2
A Can I help you?
B Yes, please. I'd like to change some money.
A Certainly, ma'am. What would you like to change?
B I'd like to change ten thousand yen into dollars, please.
A US dollars?
B Yes, please.
A We charge two percent commission.
B That's fine.
A All right ... That comes to eighty-eight dollars and eighty-eight cents.

Dialog 3
A Yes, sir?
B Check, please!
A Certainly, sir. OK, let's see. Steak sandwich, French fries, coffee. That'll be, uh, fifteen dollars and fifty cents with tax.
B Excuse me, I didn't have a steak sandwich, I had a cheeseburger. And I had a Coke, not a coffee.
A Oh, I'm sorry, sir! Wrong order! That should be ... ten seventy including tax.
B That sounds better! Can I pay by traveler's check?
A I'm sorry, sir. We don't accept traveler's checks, only cash.
B OK. There you go. Thirteen dollars. Keep the change.
A Thank you, sir.

LISTEN AND PRACTICE Listen to the dialogs and check your answers.

Dialog 1
Customer How much are these books?
Clerk They're eighteen fifty.
Customer OK, I'll take one.
Clerk How would you like to pay?
Customer Do you accept credit cards?
Clerk Yes, sir. Could I have your card, please?
Customer Here you are.

Dialog 2
Customer I'd like to change some money.
Clerk Certainly, ma'am. How much would you like to change?
Customer I'd like to change one hundred US dollars into yen, please.
Clerk OK. We charge two percent commission.
Customer Two percent? That's fine.
Clerk All right ... That comes to nine thousand, one hundred yen.

12

LISTENING Listen to the guide. Complete the notes on the itinerary. Choose the correct answer.

Mercedes Good morning. My name is Mercedes. I am your guide for the next few days on your bus trip through Southern Peru. In a few minutes, we'll leave Lima and drive south to Pisco. We'll have lunch at Pisco, at the Hotel Belen. After lunch, at around 1 o'clock, we'll take a boat to the Ballestas Islands where we hope to see some flamingos, pelicans, and sea lions. We won't land on the islands, but we will have drinks and something to eat on the boat. At 5 o'clock we'll meet up with the bus again and go onto Nazca. Finally, we'll drive to the Las Dunas Hotel for dinner.

I recommend an early night, as breakfast on Wednesday is at 6 a.m. After breakfast, the bus will take us to Nazca Airport and we'll take a short plane trip to view the Nazca Lines.

When you leave the bus, remember to take all your belongings with you. Are there any questions?

A Are we going to stop before Pisco?
Mercedes Yes. We'll take a short break en route.
B How long will we stay in Nazca? ...

LISTEN AND PRACTICE Listen to the cassette and fill in the blanks.

1 We'll stop here for 10 minutes. Please be back at the bus by 11:30.
2 Please remember to take all your belongings with you.
3 You are welcome to take photographs outside, but please do not use a flash inside the palace.
4 I have your group entry ticket. Please keep together until we are inside.
5 The afternoon is free. The bus will leave again at 5:30 p.m.
6 We'll stop in front of the palace so that you can take photographs.
7 We'll stay here for one hour to give you a chance to look around and buy souvenirs.
8 We'll meet back here at 3 o'clock.

13

LISTENING An American tourist is in a tourist information office in Mexico City. He is asking about what to do and see in Mexico. Listen to the dialog. Check the places the information officer suggests.

Information Officer This is an excellent map of the city. It shows the main bus and train routes, and of course the principal tourist attractions.
Tourist Great! So, what should I do while I'm here?
IO Well, why don't you take a city bus tour? That way you'll get a general idea of what the city has to offer.
T That sounds like a good start. But what would you suggest?
IO Well, I suggest you visit the National Palace and the Cathedral.
T OK. What about day-trips?
IO Well, you could take a day-trip to Teotihuacan. It's not too far from the city and it's an important historical site.
T Oh yeah! That's where the pyramids are!
IO That's right!
T OK. What about longer trips?
IO Well, if you have longer, you could take a 4 or 5 day excursion to Yucatan. You could visit Chichen Itza, and then go to Cancun. Cancun is one of the most beautiful beaches in the Caribbean.
T Now that sounds perfect! Can you organize that for me?
IO I can call some of the companies that run tours for you. When would you like to go?
T Maybe in a couple of days? First, I want to ...

LISTEN AND PRACTICE Listen and match the phrases.

1 Why don't you fly there to save time?
2 I suggest you stay overnight in one of the temple guesthouses.
3 I recommend you visit one of the traditional villages.
4 You could take the train one way and fly back.
5 Why don't you visit the shrines first and then go to the shopping mall?
6 Are you interested in walking tours?
7 I strongly recommend a railpass because it's a very good deal.
8 I suggest you visit the Palace this morning while it's cool, and visit the art gallery in the afternoon.

14

LISTENING Listen to the dialog. Are the sentences true or false?

Caller I'm calling about the vacation special to Thailand and Malaysia.
Travel Agent Yes. How can I help you?
C Well, I know the price is four hundred ninety-five dollars. But is there any discount for a group?
TA How many people is it for?
C At least eight, maybe ten.
TA OK. If you can get ten, there's a discount.
C How much would we save?
TA Ten percent of the cost. So about fifty dollars each.
C I see.
TA Shall I send you a brochure?
C Yes, please.
TA OK, but don't wait too long to book. Some of the tours only have a few places left.

    C I see. How many places are there on the tour leaving on Wednesday, January 8th?
  TA January 8th, Thailand and Malaysia Special. Hm ... there are only eight places left on that tour.
    C Well, I need to talk to the other people in the group.
  TA Would you like me to hold those places for you until next Thursday?
    C That would be great.
  TA Fine. I'll mail you the brochure today. Can I have your address?

LISTEN AND PRACTICE

Listen to these dialogs in a travel agency. Fill in the blanks.

Dialog 1
A Do you have any information about vacation tours in Chile?
B Yes, we do. Shall I send you some brochures?
A Yes, please.
B Could I have your name and address?

Dialog 2
A I'd like to speak to Mr. De Vito.
B I'm afraid he's in a meeting. Would you like me to take a message?
A No, that's OK, thanks. I'll call back later.

Dialog 3
A I'm sorry, I lost my itinerary.
B Don't worry. I'll send you a copy.
A That would be great.

Dialog 4
A How many nights is it for?
B It's for 3 nights, from the 12th through the 14th of August.
A I see. Just a moment, please, and I'll check for you.

15

LISTENING

Listen to the job interview and choose the correct answer.

A So you're from São Paulo, Ms. Sobral?
B Well, I was born in Rio de Janeiro. My parents moved here when I was ten.
A In your letter it says you have visited the United States.
B Yes. I spent two months there last summer. It helped my English a lot.
A Yes. Your English is very good. Now, tell me, why do you want to be a travel agent?
B I have always wanted to travel, and my teachers in high school suggested the Diploma course at the tourism school.
A Well, you have reached the end of the course now. Have you enjoyed it?
B Yes. Very much.
A What have you enjoyed most?
B Business administration classes, I guess, but also learning how to use the computer reservations system.
A I see. Which languages can you speak?
B I can speak Portuguese, obviously, a little Spanish, and some English.
A Oh really? When did you start learning English?
B Oh, in high school.
A And have you taken any English exams?
B Yes, I took the TOEFL exam last month. I'm waiting for my results ...

LISTEN AND PRACTICE

Listen and check your answers.

A Good morning. Please take a seat. Can I have your name, please?
B Yes, I'm Kyoko Tanaka.
A Thank you, Ms. Tanaka. Could you tell me a little bit about yourself?
B Well, my name is Kyoko and I'm 19 years old. I'm studying at Tokyo Air Travel College and I'll graduate next March. I hope to work in the travel industry next year.
A Good. Which languages can you speak?
B I speak Japanese and some English.
A Have you taken any exams in English?
B Yes, I took the TOEIC exam last month. But I've also taken exams in word processing and business administration.
A Oh really? How fast can you type?
B 70 words a minute.
A That's very fast! Well, thank you, Ms. Tanaka. Please wait here while I ask Mr. Takahashi, our personnel manager, to come in and see you.
B Thank you.

Word list

The translations below refer to words only as they are used in this book. The meanings of certain words will vary according to context.

◆

ENGLISH	JAPANESE	SPANISH	PORTUGUESE
(credit) card number 4	（クレジット）カード番号	número de la tarjeta (de crédito)	número do cartão
... with bath 4	風呂付の	... con baño	... com banheira
... with shower 4	シャワー付の	... con regadera (Esp. con ducha)	... com chuveiro
accept 11	受け入れる	aceptar	aceitar
accommodations 8	宿泊施設	alojamiento	alojamento
address 4	住所	dirección, domicilio	endereço
afternoon 3	午後	tarde	tarde
ago 15	前	hace (un año)	one year ago = há um ano
airport 1	空港	aeropuerto	aeroporto
aisle seat 8	通路側座席	asiento en el pasillo	lugar no corredor
always 15	ずっと	siempre	sempre
ancient 12	古代の	antiguo	antigo
appetizer 10	前菜	aperitivo, botana (Esp. tapas)	entrada
around 9	頃	alrededor	por volta das
arrival 4	到着	llegada	chegada
arrive 3	到着する	llegar	chegar
art gallery 6	美術館	galería de arte	galeria de arte
as soon as possible 7	できる限り早く	lo antes posible	logo que possível
at least 5	少なくとも	al menos	pelo menos
attraction 13	名所	atracción	atração
availability 14	空き	disponibilidad	disponibilidade
awful 9	ひどい	terrible	horrível
bag 5	かばん	bolsa	bolsa
baked potato 10	ベークド・ポテト	papa al horno (Esp. patata al horno)	batata assada
baked salmon 10	ベークド・サーモン	salmón al horno	salmão assado
bank 3	銀行	banco	banco
bar 2	バー	bar, cantina	bar
bartender (or barmaid) 2	バーテン（女性のバーテン）	mesero (Esp. camarero)	garçom (ou garçonete)
be back 7	戻る	regresar	voltar
be born 15	生まれる	nacer	nascer
be left 14	残っている	quedar	ser deixado
beach 13	海岸	playa	praia
beautiful 9	美しい	hermoso, bello	muito bonito
beer 9	ビール	cerveza	cerveja
bellhop 2	ベルボーイ	botones	boy
belongings 12	所持品	pertenencias	pertences
beverage 10	飲み物	bebida	bebida
blanket 14	毛布	cobija, manta	cobertor
board 5	搭乗	abordar	embarcar
boarding pass 5	搭乗券	tarjeta de abordaje	cartão de embarque

ENGLISH	CHINESE	THAI	KOREAN
(credit) card number 4	(信用)卡號碼	หมายเลขบัตรเครดิต	(크레디트) 카드 번호
... with bath 4	...帶浴缸	.......รวมอ่างอาบน้ำ	욕실 겸비
... with shower 4	...帶淋浴	.......รวมฝักบัว	샤워 겸비
accept 11	接受	รับ	받다
accommodations 8	住宿	ที่พัก	숙박 시설
address 4	地址	ที่อยู่	주소
afternoon 3	下午(錄音帶稿)	กลางวัน	오후
ago 15	...以前	ที่แล้ว	전에
airport 1	機場	สนามบิน	공항
aisle seat 8	機艙過道座位	ที่นั่งติดทางเดิน	통로쪽 좌석
always 15	總是，一直	เสมอ	언제나
ancient 12	古老的	โบราณ	오래된
appetizer 10	前菜(開胃菜)	อาหารหรือเครื่องดื่มเรียกน้ำย่อย	아페타이저
around 9	大約	รอบ	경에
arrival 4	抵達(名詞)	การเดินทางมาถึง	도착
arrive 3	抵達(動詞)	มาถึง	도착하다
art gallery 6	畫廊	ห้องแสดงศิลป	미술관
as soon as possible 7	盡快、盡早	เร็วที่สุด	가능한 한 빨리
at least 5	至少	อย่างน้อยที่สุด	최소한
attraction 13	景點	สิ่งดึงดูด	명승지
availability 14	有供、有售、備有	ว่าง	있는지
awful 9	真不好	แย่	아주 재미없는
bag 5	包、袋	กระเป๋า	가방
baked potato 10	烤馬鈴薯	มันฝรั่งอบ	구은 감자
baked salmon 10	烤鮭魚	ปลาซาลมอนอบ	구은 연어
bank 3	銀行	ธนาคาร	은행
bar 2	酒吧	บาร์	바아
bartender (or barmaid) 2	酒吧男掌櫃(或酒吧女掌櫃)	ผู้บริการเครื่องดื่ม	바텐더 (바메이드)
be back 7	回來	กลับมา	돌아오다
be born 15	出生	เกิด	태어나다
be left 14	還有，尚有	ทิ้งไว้	남다
beach 13	海灘	ชายหาด	해안
beautiful 9	美麗的	สวย	아름다운
beer 9	啤酒	เบียร์	맥주
bellhop 2	侍者	พนักงานขนกระเป๋า	보이
belongings 12	個人物品	ทรัพย์สมบัติ	소지품
beverage 10	飲料	เครื่องดื่ม	음료
blanket 14	毯子	ผ้าห่ม	담요
board 5	登(機)	ขึ้นเครื่องบิน	탑승하다
boarding pass 5	登機卡	บัตรผ่านขึ้นเครื่องบิน	탑승권

79

ENGLISH	JAPANESE	SPANISH	PORTUGUESE
boat 12	船	bote, barco	barco
bookstore 6	書店	librería	livraria
breakfast 3	朝食	desayuno	café da manhã
brochure 14	案内書	folleto	brochura
building 5	ビル	edificio	edifício
bus 3	バス	camión (Esp. autobús)	ônibus
bus stop 6	バス停	parada de camión (Esp. autobús)	ponto de ônibus
business administration 15	経営学	administración comercial	administração de empresas
busy 7	話し中	ocupado	ocupado
buy 9	買う	comprar	comprar
Caesar salad 10	シーザー・サラダ	ensalada César	salada César
call (*n*) 7	電話	llamada	chamada
call (*vb*) 7	電話を掛ける	llamar	chamar
call back 7	折り返し電話を掛ける	devolver la llamada	chamar de volta
caller 7	電話の掛け手	la persona que llama	chamador
car rental office 6	レンタカー取扱所	agencia de alquiler de coches	agência de aluguel de automóveis
carry 14	運ぶ	llevar	carregar
cash 4	現金	en efectivo	dinheiro
cathedral 14	大聖堂	catedral	catedral
certainly 7	承知しました	por supuesto, con mucho gusto	pois não
change money 11	両替する	cambiar dinero	trocar dinheiro
charbroiled 16 oz. steak 10	450g 炭火焼きステーキ	bistec a la parrilla de 450 gr.	filé grelhado na brasa de 450 g
charge (*vb*) 11	請求する	cobrar	cobrar
check (*n*) 11	小切手	cheque	conta
check (*vb*) 14	調べる	verificar, checar	verificar
check in 5	チェック・イン	registrarse	fazer o check in
check out 5	チェック・アウト	salir	fechar a conta
check-in clerk 8	搭乗手続き係	recepcionista	agente de tráfego
chicken in a white wine sauce 10	鶏肉の白ワインソース添え	pollo en salsa bechamel envinada	frango com molho de vinho branco
city 1	都市	ciudad	cidade
city tour 8	市内観光	tour de la ciudad	passeio turístico pela cidade
climb 12	登る	subir	subir
clock 3	時計	reloj	relógio
close 3	閉まる	cerrar	fechar
cold 14	寒い	tener frío, frío	com frio
comfortable 13	居心地の良い	cómodo	confortável
commission 11	手数料	comisión	comissão
company 1	会社	compañía	empresa
confirm 4	確認する	confirmar	confirmar
cool 13	涼しい	fresco	fresco
copy 14	コピー	copia	cópia
corner 6	角	esquina	esquina

80

ENGLISH	CHINESE	THAI	KOREAN
boat 12	船隻	เรือ	보트
bookstore 6	書店	ร้านขายหนังสือ	서점
breakfast 3	早餐	อาหารเช้า	아침식사
brochure 14	小冊子	หนังสือข้อมูล	팜플렛
building 5	樓、建築物	ตึก	빌딩
bus 3	巴士	รถประจำทาง	버스
bus stop 6	巴士站	ที่จอดรถประจำทาง	버스 정거장
business administration 15	商業管理	ฝ่ายบริหารธุรกิจ	경영학
busy 7	忙	ไม่ว่าง	통화중
buy 9	購買	ซื้อ	사다
Caesar salad 10	愷撒什錦沙律(色拉)	สลัดซีซาร์	시저 샐러드
call (n) 7	打電話〔動詞〕	โทรศัพท์	전화
call (vb) 7	電話〔名詞〕	โทร	전화하다
call back 7	回電話	โทรกลับ	나중에 다시 전화하다
caller 7	來電話者	ผู้โทร	전화한 사람
car rental office 6	租車處	สำนักงานบริการเช่ารถ	카 렌탈 오피스
carry 14	提、拿	ถือ	들다
cash 4	現金	เงินสด	현금
cathedral 14	大教堂	โบสถ์ใหญ่	성당
certainly 7	當然(可以)	แน่นอน	물론이다
change money 11	兌換貨幣	แลกเงิน	환금하다
charbroiled 16 oz. steak 10	炭烤450克重牛排	กริลสเต๊ก 450 กรัม	숯불구이 스테이크 450g
charge (vb) 11	收取	คิดเงิน	부과하다
check (n) 11	賬單	เช็ค	계산
check (vb) 14	核實、檢查	คิดเงิน	체크하다
check in 5	辦理住店手續	เช็คอิน	체크인
check out 5	辦理離店手續	เช็คเอาท์	체크아웃
check-in clerk 8	住店接待員	เสมียนเช็คอิน	체크인 직원
chicken in a white wine sauce 10	白酒露醬雞	ไก่ราดซอสไวน์ขาว	백포도주 소스를 친 닭요리
city 1	城市	เมือง	도시
city tour 8	城市觀光	ทัวร์ในเมือง	시내 관광
climb 12	攀、爬	ปีน	오르다
clock 3	時鐘	นาฬิกา	시계
close 3	關閉、休息(店)	ปิด	닫다
cold 14	冷	หนาว	추운
comfortable 13	舒適	สบาย	편안한
commission 11	手續費、佣金	ค่าป่วยการ	커미션
company 1	公司	บริษัท	회사
confirm 4	確認	ยืนยัน	확인하다
cool 13	涼爽	เย็น	시원한
copy 14	復本	สำเนา	복사
corner 6	拐角、角落	มุมถนน	코너

ENGLISH	JAPANESE	SPANISH	PORTUGUESE
cost 11	値段	costar	custar
credit card 4	クレジット・カード	tarjeta de crédito	cartão de crédito
crowded 13	混んでいる	lleno	cheio
currency 11	通貨	moneda	moeda
date 4	日付	fecha	data
day trip 8	日帰り旅行	excursión de un día	excursão de um dia
delicious 9	おいしい	delicioso	delicioso
department store 3	デパート	tienda de departamentos	loja de departamentos
departure 5	出発	salida	partida
departure lounge 8	出発ラウンジ	sala de embarque	salão de partida
dessert 10	デザート	postre	sobremesa
dinner 9	ディナー	cenar	jantar
discount 14	割引き	descuento	desconto
doctor 14	医師	médico	médico
Don't worry. 14	御心配なく	No se preocupe	Não se preocupe
double room 4	ダブルルーム	habitación doble	quarto de casal
drive 12	車で行く	manejar (Esp. conducir)	de carro
driver's license 8	運転免許証	licencia de manejar	carteira de motorista
drugstore 6	ドラッグストア	farmacia	farmácia
elevator 5	エレベーター	elevador	elevador
enjoy 5	楽しむ	disfrutar	Enjoy your flight! = Boa viagem!
entrance 6	入口	entrada	entrada
entrée 10	主菜	plato fuerte	prato principal
evening 3	夕方	tarde/noche	tarde
ever 15	今迄に	alguna vez	já
exam 15	試験	examen/prueba	prova
examination 15	試験	examen	exame
excellent 13	みごとな	excelente	excelente
exchange bureau 2	両替所	buró/oficina de cambio	casa de câmbio
excursion 8	小旅行	excursión	excursão
excuse me 6	すみません	dispénseme/perdón	por favor
expensive 9	（値段が）高い	caro	caro
experience 15	経験	experiencia	experiência
famous 13	有名な	famoso	famoso
fantastic 9	素晴らしい	fantástico	fantástico
fascinating 9	魅惑的な	fascinante	fascinante
fast 15	速く	rápido	velocidade
fasten 5	締める	abrochar	apertar
favorite 15	好きな	favorito	preferido
feel sick 14	気分が悪い	sentirse mal	sentir-se mal
fill in 8	記入する	rellenar	preencher
find 9	見つける	encontrar	encontrar
fine 13	洗練された	bueno	bom
flash 12	フラッシュ	flash	flash
flight 5	フライト	vuelo	vôo

ENGLISH	CHINESE	THAI	KOREAN
cost 11	花費	ราคา	가격은 …이다
credit card 4	信用卡	บัตรเครดิต	크레디트 카드
crowded 13	擁擠	แน่น	복잡한
currency 11	貨幣	อัตราแลกเปลี่ยน	통화
date 4	日期	วันที่	날짜
day trip 8	一日遊	ไปกลับภายในวันเดียว	당일코스
delicious 9	美味、可口	อร่อย	맛있는
department store 3	百貨商店	ห้างสรรพสินค้า	백화점
departure 5	起飛	ขาออก	출발
departure lounge 8	候機廳	ห้องผู้โดยสารขาออก	출발 대기실
dessert 10	甜食	ของหวาน	후식
dinner 9	晚餐	อาหารเย็น	만찬
discount 14	折價	ส่วนลด	할인
doctor 14	醫生	แพทย์	의사
Don't worry. 14	別擔心	ไม่ต้องห่วง	걱정하지 마시오
double room 4	雙人房	ห้องคู่	더블룸
drive 12	駕車	ขับรถ	차로 데리고 가다
driver's license 8	駕駛執照	ใบขับขี่	운전 면허증
drugstore 6	藥房	ร้านขายยา	약국
elevator 5	電梯	ลิฟท์	승강기
enjoy 5	享受	สนุก	즐기다
entrance 6	入口處	ทางเข้า	문
entrée 10	主菜	อาหารหลักของมื้อ	주식
evening 3	晚間(錄音帶稿)	ตอนเย็น	저녁
ever 15	從來	เคย	…한 적
exam 15	考試(動)	สอบ	시험
examination 15	考試(名)	การสอบ	시험
excellent 13	優異	ดีเยี่ยม	훌륭한
exchange bureau 2	外幣兌換處	ที่แลกเงิน	환전소
excursion 8	出遊	การท่องเที่ยว	짧은 여행
excuse me 6	對不起	ขอโทษ	실례합니다
expensive 9	昂貴的	แพง	비싼
experience 15	經歷、經驗	ประสบการณ์	경험
famous 13	著名的	มีชื่อเสียง	유명한
fantastic 9	好極了	ยอดเยี่ยม	매혹적인
fascinating 9	有趣極了、令人入迷的	น่าสนใจ	기막히게 좋은
fast 15	快	เร็ว	빨리
fasten 5	系上	รัดเข็มขัด	하다
favorite 15	最喜歡的	ของโปรด	좋아하는
feel sick 14	噁心	ไม่สบาย	메스껍다
fill in 8	填寫	กรอกข้อความ	기입하다
find 9	發現(名詞)、找到(動詞)	ค้นหา	생각하다
fine 13	好的	ดี	룽룽한
flash 12	閃光燈	สว่างจ้า	후래쉬
flight 5	班機	เที่ยวบิน	비행

ENGLISH	JAPANESE	SPANISH	PORTUGUESE
flight attendant 2	乗務員	aeromozo / azafata	comissária de bordo
fly 13	飛行機で行く	volar	de avião
form 8	用紙	formulario	formulário
fountain 6	噴水	fuente	fonte
free 12	自由行動	libre	livre
French fries 10	フライド・ポテト	papas fritas (a la francesa) (Esp. patatas)	batatas fritas
fresh orange juice 10	フレッシュ・オレンジジュース	jugo fresco de naranja (Esp. zumo)	suco de laranja fresco
full of 13	たくさんの	lleno de	cheio de
gate 5	ゲート	puerta	portão
general manager 7	総支配人	gerente general	gerente geral
get back 9	戻る	regresar	voltar
get up 12	起床	levantarse	levantar
give a message 7	伝言を伝える	dar un recado	dar um recado
give you a chance to 12	〜の機会を与える	permitir	lhes dar uma oportunidade de
go shopping 9	買い物に行く	ir de compras	fazer compras
good deal 13	お買い得	buen precio	econômico
graduate 15	卒業する	graduarse	formar-se
great 14	素晴らしい	fantástico	excelente
green beans 10	緑豆	ejotes (Esp. judías verdes)	vagem
greet 1	迎える	saludar	cumprimentar
greeting 13	挨拶	saludo	cumprimento
group entry ticket 12	団体入場券	boleto de entrada para grupos (Esp. billete)	ingresso de grupo
guest 4	宿泊者	huésped	hóspede
guesthouse 13	ゲストハウス	casa de huéspedes	pensão
guided tour 12	ガイド付観光	excursión guiada	visita com guia
hand luggage 8	手荷物	equipaje de mano	bagagem de mão
handshake 13	握手	dar la mano	aperto de mão
heavy 14	重い	pesado	pesado
helicopter 12	ヘリコプター	helicóptero	helicóptero
help 8	手伝う	ayuda	Deseja alguma coisa?
high school 15	高校	preparatoria	segundo grau
historical 13	歴史的な	histórico	histórico
hold 7	（電話口で）待つ	esperar	esperar na linha
hope 15	希望する	esperar	esperar
hot 9	熱い	caliente, picante	quente
hot springs 12	温泉	termas	termas
hotel 2	ホテル	hotel	hotel
house wine 10	ハウスワイン	vino de la casa	vinho da casa
I'll just check ... 3	調べてみます	Voy a checar / ver	Vou verificar ...
I'm afraid ... 7	残念ながら	Lo siento ...	Sinto muito ...
I'm sorry. 7	申し訳ありません	Discúlpeme / lo siento	Sinto muito.

ENGLISH	CHINESE	THAI	KOREAN
flight attendant 2	機務人員	พนักงานต้อนรับบนเครื่องบิน	항공기 승무원
fly 13	飛行	บิน	비행기를 타다
form 8	表格	เอกสาร	용지
fountain 6	噴泉	น้ำพุ	분수
free 12	自由活動	ว่าง	자유시간
French fries 10	炸薯條	มันฝรั่งทอดกรอบ	후렌치 후라이
fresh orange juice 10	鮮橙汁	น้ำส้มสด	신선한 오렌지 주스
full of 13	充滿	อิ่ม	...이 많은
gate 5	門	ประตูทางออก	게이트
general manager 7	總經理	ผู้จัดการทั่วไป	총지배인
get back 9	回來	กลับมา	돌아오다
get up 12	起來	ลุกขึ้น	기상하다
give a message 7	留言	ทิ้งข้อความไว้	메시지를 전하다
give you a chance to 12	讓你有機會...	ให้โอกาส	...할 기회를 주다
go shopping 9	購物	ไปซื้อของ	쇼핑하러 가다
good deal 13	很值、貨真價實	ราคาดี	값이 싸다
graduate 15	畢業	เรียนจบ	졸업하다
great 14	太好了	ดีเยี่ยม	아주 좋다
green beans 10	青豆	ถั่วฝักยาว	그린 빈
greet 1	歡迎	ทักทาย	인사하다
greeting 13	見面禮	การทักทาย	인사
group entry ticket 12	集體票	ตั๋วเข้าเป็นกลุ่ม	단체 입장표
guest 4	客人	แขก	손님
guesthouse 13	賓館	เกสท์เฮาส์	여관
guided tour 12	導遊旅遊	ทัวร์ไกด์	안내인 딸린 관광
hand luggage 8	手提行李	กระเป๋าถือ	손가방
handshake 13	握手	จับมือ	악수
heavy 14	重	หนัก	무거운
helicopter 12	直升飛機	เฮลีคอปเตอร์	헬리콥터
help 8	幫助	ช่วย	돕다
high school 15	高中	โรงเรียนระดับมัธยมศึกษา	고등학교
historical 13	歷史性的	สำคัญทางประวัติศาสตร์	역사적인
hold 7	等一下	ถือ	기다리다
hope 15	希望	หวัง	희망하다
hot 9	熱的、燙的	ร้อน	매운
hot springs 12	溫泉	น้ำพุร้อน	온천
hotel 2	旅館	โรงแรม	호텔
house wine 10	本店自備酒	ไวน์ของสถานที่นั้น	하우스 와인
I'll just check ... 3	我馬上查一查...	เดี๋ยวขอตรวจดูก่อน	...을 잠깐 체크 해보겠습니다
I'm afraid ... 7	我恐怕...	ฉันเกรงว่า.......	유감스럽지만
I'm sorry. 7	對不起、很抱歉	ฉันเสียใจ	미안합니다

ENGLISH	JAPANESE	SPANISH	PORTUGUESE
immediately 5	直ちに	inmediatamente	imediatamente
immigration officer 8	出入国管理官	oficial de inmigración	funcionário da imigração
important 13	重要な	importante	importante
including tax 11	税込み	incluyendo el impuesto	incluindo o imposto
industry 15	業界	industria turística	setor
inside 12	屋内	dentro / adentro	dentro (de)
interested in 14	〜に興味がある	estar interesado	interessado em
interesting 9	興味深い	interesante	interessante
interview 15	面接	entrevista	entrevista
introduce oneself 1	自己紹介する	presentarse	apresentar-se
introduction 1	紹介	presentación	apresentação
island 12	島	isla	ilha
itinerary 12	旅行日程表	programa / itinerario	itinerário
Just a moment ... 3	少々お待ち下さい	Un momentito ...	Um momento ...
keep together 12	行動を共にする	No se separen	mantenham-se juntos
land (*vb*) 12	上陸する	desembarcar	desembarcar
language 15	言語	idioma	língua
last 15	昨年の	último	passado
later 14	後ほど	más tarde, después	mais tarde
leave 3	出発する	salir	partir
luggage check 8	手荷物一時預り所	depósito de equipaje	depósito de bagagem
line 7	回線	línea	linha
lively 13	にぎやかな	animado / alegre	animado
local check 11	現地通貨の小切手	cheque local	cheque local
look around 12	あちこち見てまわる	dar una ojeada	dar uma olhada
lost 14	なくした	perder	perdi
lost and found office 6	遺失物取扱所	oficina de objetos perdidos	seção de perdidos e achados
lunch 3	昼食	comida, almuerzo	almoço
mail 14	郵送する	enviar	enviar
main 6	主な	principal	principal
map 1	地図	mapa	mapa
market 12	マーケット	mercado	mercado
meat 10	肉料理	carne	carne
medicine 8	内服薬	medicina	remédio
meet 1	会う	conocer	conhecer
meet (2) 12	出迎える	encontrar, reunirse	encontrar
meeting 14	会議	reunión	reunião
melon with ham 10	生ハムメロン	melón con jamón	melão com presunto
menu 10	メニュー	menú, carta	menu
method of payment 4	支払い方法	método de pago	método de pagamento
midday 3	正午	mediodía	meio-dia
midnight 3	深夜12時	medianoche	meia-noite
mineral water 10	ミネラルウォーター	agua mineral	água mineral
month 15	月	mes	mês

ENGLISH	CHINESE	THAI	KOREAN
immediately 5	立即	ทันที	즉시
immigration officer 8	移民局官員	เจ้าหน้าที่ตรวจคนเข้าเมือง	이민국 직원
important 13	重要的	สำคัญ	중요한
including tax 11	含稅	รวมภาษี	세금을 포함해서
industry 15	工業、行業	อุตสาหกรรม	업계
inside 12	在...裡	ข้างใน	안에
interested in 14	對...有興趣	สนใจ	...에 괌심이 있다
interesting 9	有趣的	น่าสนใจ	흥미있는
interview 15	面談	สัมภาษณ์	인터뷰
introduce oneself 1	自我介紹	แนะนำตัว	자신을 소개하다
introduction 1	介紹	การแนะนำตัว	소개
island 12	島	เกาะ	섬
itinerary 12	日程安排	แผนการเดินทาง	여정
Just a moment ... 3	請稍候	รอประเดี๋ยว	잠깐만..
keep together 12	別分散	เก็บไว้ด้วยกัน	모여 있다
land (*vb*) 12	著陸	ลงจอด	착륙하다
language 15	語言	ภาษา	언어
last 15	上一個	ท้ายสุด	지난
later 14	後來、稍後	ที่หลัง	나중에
leave 3	離開	ออกเดินทาง	출발하다
luggage check 8	行李寄存處	ที่ฝากกระเป๋า	보관시키는 짐
line 7	線	แถว	전화
lively 13	活躍的	มีชีวิตชีวา	활기 있는
local check 11	當地賬單	เช็คของประเทศนั้น ๆ	국내 수표
look around 12	四周看看、逛一逛	เที่ยวดู	둘러보다
lost 14	丟失	ของหาย	잃어 버리다
lost and found office 6	失物招領處	สำนักงานตรวจดูของหาย	분실물 취급소
lunch 3	午餐	อาหารกลางวัน	점심 식사
mail 14	郵寄	จดหมาย	우편으로 보내다
main 6	主要的	ประตูใหญ่	정
map 1	地圖	แผนที่	지도
market 12	市場	ตลาด	시장
meat 10	肉	ประเภทของเนื้อ	육식
medicine 8	藥品	ยา	약
meet 1	會見、見到	พบ	만나다
meet (2) 12	接	การพบ	만나다
meeting 14	會議	การพบปะ	미팅
melon with ham 10	火腿甜瓜	แตงกับแฮม	햄이 든 멜론
menu 10	菜單	รายการอาหาร	메뉴
method of payment 4	付款方式	จ่ายโดย	지불 방법
midday 3	中午	เที่ยงวัน	정오
midnight 3	午夜	เที่ยงคืน	자정
mineral water 10	礦泉水	น้ำแร่	미네랄 워터
month 15	月	เดือน	달

ENGLISH	JAPANESE	SPANISH	PORTUGUESE
more 14	もっと	más	mais
morning 3	午前	mañana	manhã
mountain 13	山	montaña	montanha
museum 14	博物館	museo	museu
nationality 15	国籍	nacionalidad	nacionalidade
nearby 9	近くの	cerca	próximo
next 14	来週の	al lado de	próximo
night 4	泊	noche	noite
night-club 13	ナイトクラブ	centro nocturno	boate
occupation 15	職業	ocupación, empleo	profissão
one way 3	片道	ida	ida
open 3	開く	abrir	abrir
order (n) 10	注文	pedido	pedido
order (vb) 9	注文する	pedir	pedir
outside 5	〜の外	delante de	ao lado de
over 13	〜の上の	sobre	sobre
over there 12	あそこに	ahí/allí	lá adiante
overseas 15	海外	en el extranjero	no exterior
painkiller 14	鎮痛剤	analgésico	analgésico
palace 13	宮殿	palacio	palácio
parking lot 6	駐車場	estacionamiento (Esp. aparcamiento)	estacionamento
passenger 8	乗客	pasajero	passageiro
passport 5	パスポート	pasaporte	passaporte
pasta 9	パスタ	pasta	massa
pay 11	支払う	pagar	pagar
peaceful 13	穏やかな	tranquilo, callado	tranqüila
percent 11	パーセント	por ciento, porcentaje	por cento
personnel manager 15	人事部長	gerente de personal	gerente de pessoal
picnic 12	ピクニック	picnic	piquenique
place 13	座席	lugar	lugar
place (2) 14	場所	lugar, sitio	local
plane 5	飛行機	avión	avião
police 14	警察	policía	polícia
post office 3	郵便局	correo, oficina de correos	correio
put 5	入れる	poner	pôr
put somebody through 7	電話をつなぐ	comunicar	fazer a ligação
pyramid 13	ピラミッド	pirámide	pirâmide
quiet 9	静かな	tranquilo	calmo
railpass 13	列車の乗車券	pase ferroviario	passe de trem
ready 5	用意して	listo	na mão
really 14	本当に	realmente	realmente
reception desk 5	受付	recepción	balcão de recepção
receptionist 2	受付係	recepcionista	recepcionista

ENGLISH	CHINESE	THAI	KOREAN
more 14	更多的	เอามาเพิ่ม	더
morning 3	早晨	ตอนเช้า	오전
mountain 13	上山	ภูเขา	산
museum 14	博物館	พิพิธภัณฑ์	박물관
nationality 15	國籍	สัญชาติ	국적
nearby 9	附近	ใกล้	근처의
next 14	下一個	ต่อไป	다음
night 4	夜	กลางคืน	밤
night-club 13	夜總會	ไนท์คลับ	나이트 클럽
occupation 15	職業	อาชีพ	직업
one way 3	單程	เที่ยวเดียว	편도
open 3	開(門)、營業中	เปิด	열다
order (*n*) 10	點的菜肴	สั่ง	주문
order (*vb*) 9	點菜	สั่ง	주문하다
outside 5	在...外	ข้างนอก	밖에
over 13	在...上面	บน	위의
over there 12	在那裡	ตรงโน้น	저기
overseas 15	外國	ต่างประเทศ	외국
painkiller 14	止痛劑	ยาแก้ปวด	진통제
palace 13	宮殿	พระราชวัง	궁
parking lot 6	停車場	ที่จอดรถ	주차장
passenger 8	乘客	ผู้โดยสาร	여객
passport 5	護照	หนังสือเดินทาง	여권
pasta 9	意大利麵食	พาสต้า	파스타
pay 11	付款	จ่ายเงิน	지불하다
peaceful 13	安寧的	เงียบสงบ	평화로운
percent 11	百分比	เปอร์เซนต์	퍼센트
personnel manager 15	人事經理	ผู้จัดการส่วนบุคคล	인사 부장
picnic 12	野餐	ปิคนิค	피크닉
place 13	位置	สถานที่	자리(2)
place (2) 14	地方	สถานที่	장소
plane 5	飛機	เครื่องบิน	비행기
police 14	警察	ตำรวจ	경찰
post office 3	郵局	ที่ทำการไปรษณีย์	우체국
put 5	放	สวมใส่ต่อ	놓다
put somebody through 7	給...轉(電話)	ต่อสายให้	연결해 주다
pyramid 13	金字塔	ปิรามิด	피라미드
quiet 9	安靜的	เงียบ	조용한
railpass 13	火車通票	ตั๋วรถไฟ	레일 패스
ready 5	準備好	พร้อม	준비된
really 14	真的	จริง ๆ	정말
reception desk 5	接待處	ที่ต้อนรับ	프론트
receptionist 2	接待員	พนักงานต้อนรับ	접수계원

ENGLISH	JAPANESE	SPANISH	PORTUGUESE
recommend 9	勧める	recomendar	recomendar
reference number 4	照会番号	número de referencia	número de referência
relax 13	くつろぐ	descansar	relaxar
remember 12	忘れずに〜する	no olvidarse	lembrar-se
reservation 4	予約	reserva	reserva
reserve 8	予約する	reservar	reservar
restaurant 2	レストラン	restaurante	restaurante
restrooms 6	化粧室	baño (Esp. servicios)	banheiros
roast beef 10	ローストビーフ	carne asada, rosbif	carne assada
room type 4	部屋の形式	tipo de habitación	tipo de quarto
round trip 3	往復	viaje de ida y vuelta	ida e volta
ruins 13	廃虚	ruinas	ruínas
save time 13	時間を節約する	ahorrar tiempo	economizar tempo
scales 8	秤	báscula	balança
science 14	科学	ciencia	ciência
scuba diving 13	スキューバ・ダイビング	buceo (Esp. submarinismo)	mergulho
seat 8	座席	asiento	lugar
seatbelt 5	シートベルト	cinturón de seguridad	cinto de segurança
send 14	送る	enviar	enviar
serve 3	（食事を）出す	servir	servido
shopping mall 6	ショッピング・モール	centro comercial	shopping mall
show 9	ショー	show	show
shrine 13	神社	templo, santuario	santuário
side order 10	追加注文の料理	acompañamiento	acompanhamento
side salad 10	追加注文のサラダ	con ensalada	salada
sight 13	光景	espectáculo	espetáculo
sign 8	署名する	firmar	assinar
single room 4	シングルルーム	habitación individual	quarto de solteiro
site 13	遺跡	lugar, zona	monumento
smoke 5	タバコを吸う	fumar	fumar
snack 12	軽食	botana (Esp. tentempié)	lanche
soft drink 10	ソフトドリンク	refrescos	refrigerante
someone 14	誰か	alguien	alguém
soup of the day 10	本日のスープ	sopa del día	sopa do dia
souvenir 9	お土産	souvenir, recuerdo	lembrança
spell 7	つづりを言う	deletrear	soletrar
spend 9	お金を費やす	gastar	gastar
station 6	駅	estación	estação
stay 12	滞在する	quedarse	dormir
stay overnight 12	一泊する	pasar la noche	passar a noite
stop 12	止まる	parar	parar
stores 3	店	tienda	loja
strongly 13	強く	mucho, realmente	seriamente
subway 9	地下鉄	metro	metrô
suggest 9	提案する	sugerir	sugerir
summer 15	夏	verano	verão
sunrise 13	日の出	salida del sol	nascer do sol
sure 8	もちろん	sí	pois não
swimming pool 6	水泳プール	alberca (Esp. piscina)	piscina

90

ENGLISH	CHINESE	THAI	KOREAN
recommend 9	推薦	แนะนำ	추천하다
reference number 4	參號	หมายเลขอ้างอิง	수표번호
relax 13	放鬆	พักผ่อน	쉬다
remember 12	記住	อย่าลืม	잊지말다
reservation 4	預訂(名詞)	สำรองที่	예약
reserve 8	預訂(動詞)	จอง	예약하다
restaurant 2	餐廳、餐館	ร้านอาหาร	레스토랑
restrooms 6	盥洗間、休息室、衛生間	ห้องน้ำ	화장실
roast beef 10	烤牛排	เนื้ออบ	로스트 비프
room type 4	房間類型	แบบของห้อง	객실형
round trip 3	雙程	ไปกลับ	일주 여행
ruins 13	遺址	โบราณสถาน	유적
save time 13	節省時間	ประหยัดเวลา	시간을 절약하다
scales 8	天平	ที่ชั่งน้ำหนัก	저울
science 14	科學	วิทยาศาสตร์	과학
scuba diving 13	斯庫巴潛水	ดำน้ำลึก	스쿠버 다이빙
seat 8	座位	ที่นั่ง	좌석
seatbelt 5	安全帶	เข็มขัดนิรภัย	좌석 벨트
send 14	寄、送	ส่ง	보내다
serve 3	供應	บริการ	서브하다
shopping mall 6	購物中心	ห้างสรรพสินค้า	쇼핑 몰
show 9	表演	การแสดง	쇼
shrine 13	祭壇	ศาลเจ้า	사당
side order 10	配菜	อาหารจานเคียง	추가 요리
side salad 10	副食沙律(色拉)	สลัดจานเคียง	추가 샐러드
sight 13	景致	สถานที่ท่องเที่ยว	광경
sign 8	簽字	เซ็นชื่อ	서명하다
single room 4	單人房	ห้องเดี่ยว	싱글룸
site 13	遺址	สถานที่	유적
smoke 5	吸煙	สูบบุหรี่	담배를 피우다
snack 12	小食	ของว่าง	간식
soft drink 10	軟飲料	เครื่องดื่ม	음료수
someone 14	某人	บางคน	누가
soup of the day 10	當日特備湯	ซุปประจำวัน	오늘의 스프
souvenir 9	紀念品	ของที่ระลึก	기념품
spell 7	拼寫	สะกด	스펠링을 말하다
spend 9	花費	ใช้จ่าย	소비하다
station 6	火車站	สถานี	역
stay 12	住、留宿	พักอยู่	묵다
stay overnight 12	留宿一夜、下榻一夜	ค้างคืน	일박하다
stop 12	停住	หยุด	멈추다
stores 3	商店	เก็บไว้	상점
strongly 13	強烈、竭力	รุนแรง	강력하개
subway 9	地鐵	รถไฟใต้ดิน	지하철
suggest 9	建議	แนะนำ	제안하다
summer 15	夏季	ฤดูร้อน	여름
sunrise 13	日出	พระอาทิตย์ขึ้น	일출
sure 8	肯定、可以	แน่นอน	물론이다
swimming pool 6	游泳池	สระว่ายน้ำ	수영장

ENGLISH	JAPANESE	SPANISH	PORTUGUESE
tag 5	付け札	etiqueta	etiqueta
take a message 7	伝言を受ける	dejar un recado	deixar recado
telephone 6	電話	teléfono	telefone
temple 13	寺院	templo	templo
terminal 5	ターミナル	terminal	terminal
That comes to ... 11	〜になる	El total es...	Isto vai dar ...
That's fine. 4	結構です	Está bien	Está bem.
theatre (US theater) 6	劇場	teatro	teatro
through 5	〜を通り抜けて	por	pela
time 3	時刻	hora	hora
timetable 3	時刻表	programa, horario	horário
tiring 9	疲れる	cansado	cansativo
tomato juice 10	トマトジュース	jugo de (ji) tomate (Esp. zumo)	suco de tomate
tomorrow 14	明日	mañana	amanhã
tonight 12	今晩	esta noche	hoje à noite
top 12	頂上	cima	topo
tour company representative 1	旅行会社現地係員	representante de la agencia turística	representante da empresa de turismo
tour group 1	団体旅行客	grupo de turistas	grupo turístico
tour guide 2	ツアー・ガイド	guía de turistas (Esp. guía de turismo)	guia turístico
tour operator 1	ツアー・オペレーター	operador turístico	empresa de viagens
tour rep 1	旅行会社現地係員	representante turístico	representante turístico
tourism 15	観光事業	turismo	turismo
tourist 1	旅行者	turista	turista
tourist information office 2	ツーリスト・インフォメーション事務所	oficina de información turística	agência de informações turísticas
tourist information officer 2	ツーリスト・インフォメーション職員	oficial de información turística	funcionário de agência de turismo
traditional 13	伝統的な	tradicional	tradicional
train 3	列車	tren	trem
training 15	トレーニング	entrenamiento (Esp. capacitación)	treinamento
transfer 12	移動	transferencia	transferência
travel agency 2	旅行代理店	agencia de viajes	agência de viagens
travel clerk 2	旅行業者	agente de viajes	funcionário de agência de viagens
traveler's check 4	トラベラーズ・チェック	cheques de viajero	cheque de viagem
type 15	タイプする	tipo	tipo
unattended 5	放置する	desatendidas	sem supervisão
until 6	〜まで	hasta	até
use 12	使う	usar	usar
vacation special 14	休暇用特別プラン	oferta especial de vacaciones	oferta especial de férias
vegetable 10	野菜	verduras	legume
village 12	村落	pueblo	aldeia

ENGLISH	CHINESE	THAI	KOREAN
tag 5	標籤	ป้ายชื่อ	짐표
take a message 7	記下留言	ฝากข้อความ	메시지를 남기다
telephone 6	電話	โทรศัพท์	전화
temple 13	寺院	วัด	사원
terminal 5	終點站、總站	ชานชลา	터미날
That comes to ... 11	一共...	รวมทั้งหมด.......	합계는...이다
That's fine. 4	好	ตกลง	예, 좋습니다.
theatre (US theater) 6	電影院	โรงละคร	극장
through 5	通過	ผ่าน	통해
time 3	時間	เวลา	시간
timetable 3	時刻表	ตารางเวลา	시간표
tiring 9	令人疲勞	น่าเบื่อ	힘든
tomato juice 10	蕃茄醬	น้ำมะเขือเทศ	토마토 주스
tomorrow 14	明天	พรุ่งนี้	내일
tonight 12	今晚	คืนนี้	오늘 밤
top 12	頂	บนยอด	정상
tour company representative 1	旅遊公司代表	ตัวแทนบริษัทท่องเที่ยว	여행사 직원
tour group 1	旅遊團體	กรุ๊ปทัวร์	관광 그룹
tour guide 2	導遊	คนนำเที่ยว	관광 가이드
tour operator 1	旅行社	ผู้จัดนำเที่ยว	투어 오퍼레이터
tour rep 1	旅遊代表	ตัวแทนบริษัทท่องเที่ยว	여행사 직원
tourism 15	旅遊業	การท่องเที่ยว	관광
tourist 1	遊客	นักท่องเที่ยว	관광객
tourist information office 2	遊客問詢處	สำนักงานท่องเที่ยว	관광 안내소
tourist information officer 2	遊客問詢處職員	เจ้าหน้าที่สำนักงานท่องเที่ยว	관광 안내소 직원
traditional 13	傳統的	เป็นประเพณี	전통적인
train 3	火車	ฝึกอบรม	기차
training 15	訓練	การฝึกอบรม	트레이닝
transfer 12	轉	โอนถ่าย	이동
travel agency 2	旅行社(代理)	บริษัทท่องเที่ยว	여행사
travel clerk 2	旅行社職員	พนักงานบริษัทท่องเที่ยว	여행사 직원
traveler's check 4	旅行支票	ตั๋วแลกเงินเดินทาง	여행자 수표
type 15	打字	แบบ	타이프 치다
unattended 5	無人值守、無人看管	ไม่มีคนเฝ้า	지키지 않고
until 6	直到	จนกระทั่ง	까지
use 12	使用	ใช้	사용하다
vacation special 14	特價旅遊計劃	ทัวร์วันหยุดราคาพิเศษ	특별 휴가 프로그램
vegetable 10	蔬菜	ผัก	채식
village 12	村莊	หมู่บ้าน	마을

ENGLISH	JAPANESE	SPANISH	PORTUGUESE
visa 5	ビザ	visa	visto
visit 9	見学する	visita	visitar
waiter (or waitress) 2	ウェイター（ウェイトレス）	mesero (Esp. camarero)	garçom (ou garçonete)
walk 9	歩く	caminar	caminhar
walking tour 13	ウォーキング・ツアー	excursión a pie	passeio turístico a pé
wallet 14	札入れ	cartera, billetera	carteira
watch 14	腕時計	reloj	relógio
weekend 13	週末	fin de semana	fim-de-semana
welcome 1	ようこそ	bienvenido	Bem-vindos
window seat 8	窓側座席	asiento con ventanilla	lugar na janela
winter 15	冬	invierno	inverno
wonderful 9	すばらしい	maravilloso	maravilhoso
word processing 15	ワープロ	procesamiento de palabras (Esp. de textos)	processamento de texto
year 15	年	año	ano
you are welcome to ... 12	自由に〜してよい	puede.../está permitido	é permitido

ENGLISH	CHINESE	THAI	KOREAN
visa 5	簽證	วีซ่า	비자
visit 9	訪問、參觀	การเยี่ยมเยือน	방문하다
waiter (or waitress) 2	侍者(女侍者)	พนักงานบริการ	웨이터 (여종업원)
walk 9	步行	เดิน	걷다
walking tour 13	徒步觀光	ทัวร์เดิน	도보 관광
wallet 14	錢包	กระเป๋าใส่เงิน	지갑
watch 14	手錶	นาฬิกาข้อมือ	시계
weekend 13	週末	วันหยุดสุดสัปดาห์	주말
welcome 1	歡迎	ต้อนรับ	환영하다
window seat 8	靠窗座位	ที่นั่งติดหน้าต่าง	창가 좌석
winter 15	冬季	ฤดูหนาว	겨울
wonderful 9	很好的、令人嘆止	เยี่ยม	훌륭한
word processing 15	文字處理	เวอร์ด โพรเซสซิ่ง	워드프로세싱
year 15	年	ปี	년
you are welcome to ... 12	歡迎你來......、歡迎光臨......	ขอต้อนรับสู่	...을 해도 좋습니다.